# MORE THAN A HAIR JOURNEY:

## The Black Woman's Guide to Self-Love & Loc Maintenance

Written by Keisha Charmaine Felix

"More Than A Hair Journey: The Black Woman's Guide to Self-Love and Loc Maintenance"

Copyright © 2017 Keisha Charmaine Felix

All rights reserved.

No parts of this book may be used or reproduced in any manner whatsoever without written permission from the author.

Photography by Chioma Nwana @foundchichi

Cover Art by Curtis Bryant @curtisbryant_

Edited by Joanne Pamela Massiah Felix

ISBN-13: 978-1540380814
ISBN-10: 1540380815

To my future daughters,

May you allow yourselves to love yourselves without resistance, with divine light

# TABLE OF CONTENTS

## PART I: My Self-Love Journey

Introduction…………………………………………..9

Do Black Girls Really Rock?......................................15

Black & Beautiful…………………………………….21

Reflections of Ourselves……………………………26

Self-Love Is… …………………………………….....31

Self-Love in Question………………………………37

Growth from Failure………………………………...44

How to Self-Love……………………………………48

Balance………………………………………………..52

From Rejection to Obsession………………………..60

End of a Relationship is Not a Failure……………...66

More Than a Hair Journey…………………………..69

Aaron Johnson……………………………………….73

Style, What Are You Protecting?...............................80

Trust You……………………………………………..84

Loc Journeys for Self-Love………………………….87

Locs & Sex Appeal…………………………………...91

Body Party……………………………………...96

Facing Fears & Indecision……………………...101

Powerful Beyond Measure……………………..105

Think Negative Thoughts……………………...109

The Consequences of Self-Love………………..114

Sweet Solitude………………………………....118

Feminine Energy……………………………....122

I Am Well……………………………………..126

## PART II: Loc Maintenance Tips

Love, Light & Locs…………………………....158

Why Am I So Passionate About Locs……………160

Quiz: Should You Loc Your Hair?……………...162

What Are Locs? & How Are They Formed?……...169

Starting Locs with Healthy Hair…………………171

Myths Debunked………………………………173

Shrinkage……………………………………...180

Washing Locs………………………………….183

Mildew & Drying Locs………………………...186

Root Maintenance……………………………..188

Moisturizing…………………………………...191

Hot Oil Treatments vs. Conditioners................193

Bedtime Maintenance...................................195

Top 3 Loc Enemies.......................................197

Product Build-up..........................................197

Lint.............................................................201

Frizz...........................................................205

Lumps........................................................210

Thinning, Breakage & Bald Spots....................212

Hairline & Edges Care..................................215

Exercise.....................................................217

Hair Color..................................................219

10 Tips for Hair Growth...............................221

Loc Removal..............................................224

Glossary....................................................226

About the Author........................................229

Contributors..............................................230

"To me, self-love is not a destination. The journey is not some linear path to the finish line. Self-love is more like the weather, cyclical like the seasons. Life is about balance. Nothing will grow without plenty rainfall."

-Keisha Charmaine Felix, 25.

@killadoesthat

# PREFACE

Tons of insecurities have risen to the surface while writing this book. I was questioning myself constantly throughout the entire process. *Keisha, you write for fun, what makes you think you're an author?* This is a legitimate question! Authors tend to take a shot of Jack with their coffee and I'm an herbal tea kind of gal. *Keisha, you are 25 years old, who do you think you are advising anybody about life?* I have a point here too. Is the human brain even fully developed at 25? *Keisha, you're not perfect. What makes you an expert on self-love?* That's true, I'm not perfect, I hardly even pair off my socks. What am I doing, telling anybody how to get their lives together if I can't even keep my socks together!?

Lucky for us all, I am not writing this book with the disposition that I have it all figured out. I am not pretending to be *flawless* in the least. In fact, I want it to be understood that I did NOT wake up like this. I actually wake up every morning, or afternoon, in efforts to accept myself more and more, *flaws and all!*

One thing I learned a bit about while writing this book is that I shouldn't take myself too seriously. Fear, worry, shame, guilt and embarrassment are incredibly debilitating. So many of us live our lives in constant apprehension and doubt because we don't want to take the wrong step. Take the step! If it turns out to be a misstep, it's okay. I've made a ton of poor decisions in my life, I can admit it, but mistakes are filled with purpose. I often beat myself up about some of the things I went through but there is always a lesson in a mistake. It's up to you to see the value in your mistakes.

In writing this book, I learned that my voice is valuable. I'm not writing anyone's bible but I'm writing my perspective. What I have on my mind and in my heart to say matters, so I can't always second guess myself or people-please. I've come a very long way and I have gathered the tools to go much further. I am not claiming to have reached the highest height of self-love, if there is even such a place. I believe self-love to be somewhat of a cyclical journey and not a linear one. It's not a race, it's not a competition. It's a constant personal journey of self-discovery and re-discovery over one's lifetime.

Most importantly, I learned that I am stronger than I'd ever given myself credit for. The year 2016 has been by far the most trying year of my life. I've had a cloud of negativity, pain and self-doubt raining over me for the bulk of the year. I felt as though some entity wanted to see my demise but maybe it wanted to push me to reach a level of greatness I hadn't yet reached. I believe God sees more in me than I see myself. While working on this book, I had to constantly remind myself to keep my faith strong and write. *Keisha, keep on writing until you've written all the words in your heart to be immortalized in your first book.*

This book is written from a young heterosexual black woman's experience. I respect that all of my readers may not fit this description in part or at all, but please read with an open mind and I promise all will be able to pull from my experiences shared and benefit from the advice I have to offer from my acquired wisdom. It is clear my intention is that black women read and benefit from this book however I encourage men and women of all races to read this book to get the perspective of someone other than their own. Part I is about my self-love journey while Part II is written to anyone who is interested in learning about loc maintenance.

I get super defensive when people try to minimize the significance of hair for black women. People think black women over value their hair but I believe most people ignore the history of black hair in America, so they don't understand why we value it so much. Our hair has always been policed. We were always told that our hair, needs to be covered, it needs to be straightened, don't get it wet, don't sweat it out, don't let it frizz up. Make sure it doesn't look too ethnic so you can get a job. Make sure it's long so you can get a man.

In the past ten years, there has been a significant rise in the number of black women who decided to ignore outside opinions and wear their hair in its natural texture. Some women chose to do a big chop (BC), shave their head or cut it very low. Other women choose to transition to natural by growing their hair out and gradually cutting off the permanently straightened ends. We have so many different reasons for deciding to embark on a natural hair journey but most of us don't realize that because of the role that hair plays in a black woman's life, a natural hair journey becomes a self-love journey.

I've been documenting my loc journey on YouTube since I started my locs in 2010. I remember filming mostly over summer break and winter break when I was home from college, and using a webcam in my dorm and a broken camera in my home bathroom with terrible lighting. Those videos are embarrassing, for sure, but I keep them public so that people can still see how far I have come, production wise, and my hair growth. Bless my viewers who were subscribed to me since then. Thanks for sticking around for my evolution. I remember being a senior in college in 2013 when I finally hit 1,000 subscribers. I started monetizing my videos and once I graduated. I learned more about filming and editing, so that I could up the quality of my presentation.

Slowly but surely, I grew a large following over the years as I would share hair updates, products I liked, styles I tried and different techniques of maintaining my hair. I learned a lot about taking care of locs through obsessive research, taking care of my own locs, taking care of a couple of my loved ones' locs and maintaining clients' locs during undergrad.

I started giving advice on my YouTube channel as I would get so many questions daily. Now that I have over 400 videos on YouTube, it can be difficult to navigate my channel and find what it is you are looking for. So, I have written a very useful guide that will be beneficial for beginners who haven't even decided if they want to loc their hair, and for seasoned veterans who want a greater understanding of some of the different ways they can maintain their locs.

Thank you so much for valuing my thoughts, my words, my voice. I am enough. As are you. Have a blessed journey =.)

"I don't follow anyone's standards. I define LIFE & BEAUTY on my own terms."

-Keisha Charmaine Felix, 25.

@killadoesthat

# DO BLACK GIRLS REALLY ROCK?

Are you familiar with this feeling? That chill that creeps through your body when you feel a sudden emotion that instantly overwhelms you. The same chill you feel when you witness a car crash. The same chill you feel when you open a heart-breaking text message. The same chill you feel when you realize a painful truth after some retrospection. I felt a chill when I signed onto Facebook one evening back in college.

The very first Black Girls Rock show was airing and it was a trending topic. As I scrolled through my newsfeed to see what my friends were doing to procrastinate, much like myself, I noticed a status written by one of my male Facebook friends. He was not my friend in real life, just a guy I met in Junior High. It's important to make the distinction between real life friends and Facebook friends. There's a world of a difference. His status stated "Why do they have a Black Girls Rock award show!? There's no award show for any other demographic, this is pointless!" Reading those words, especially coming from a black male, was very disheartening. The chills swept over the hairs on my skin and sunk deep into my bones. It made my stomach hurt. Here we go with this "all lives matter" rhetoric.

In America, black girls are conditioned to have poor self-esteem. Black girls who have loved themselves to a state of high confidence levels have done so with great resistance and opposition. We go through many lengths to learn to love ourselves since we are bombarded with so much propaganda in the media and negative talk in our own homes that teach us to hate ourselves subliminally. We have our value degraded by institutionalized and overt racism and sexism. The media often shows us we aren't beautiful, talented or smart enough by not adequately representing us in TV and movies. We are disproportionately abandoned more than any other demographic, to raise families on our own.

Didn't he know all of this? Are black women so good at *faking the funk* that he could believe we aren't hurting? Is this how most black men feel, that black girls are not deserving of the empowerment that such an award show could provide? Black men and women should be supporting each other.

The black nuclear family has been destroyed strategically for hundreds of years. Since we were separated from our loved ones on the auction block once we were enslaved, to the new slavery of mass incarceration for minor drug offenses. The psychological effects of slavery are strong. It's in our

DNA, passed on generations beyond emancipation. I believe that the enslavement of Africans in America resulted in millions of black people being content with mediocrity and complacency, with inferiority complexes, even within our own race today. Slavery in America has caused a divide between black man and black woman as well as light skinned and dark skinned. It will take a lot of serious and dedicated efforts to deconstruct our socialization and rebuild our sense of community and adequate familial foundations.

Modern day black women strive to be in certain financial positions so that we can be independent if our men leave us and our children to fend for ourselves. This in turn further diminishes the value of black fathers and the black family. Black women are made to feel that we need to compete with other black women, for the attention of our men. This essentially destroys unity among black women. Many of these struggles are not exclusive to black women. However women of color are affected significantly more as double minorities. We have to deal with the issues that come with the territory of being black and being women in America.

With all that said, the plight of black girls isn't easy. Consider how so many of us are raised fatherless, in preparation for being 'never married' and often in abusive situations, forcing us to grow up quickly. It is important to give us that reminder that we are important and we can grow up and positively impact the world. Since my Facebook friend didn't know, I'm glad he asked somebody. Black girls DO rock and the world should act accordingly.

"I am my own standard of beauty. I create beauty within first, then I channel all that love to positively influence everyone I come in contact with. That is the power of self-love."

-Nardia Brown, 31.

@kayajourney

"Beauty is in the imagination. If you believe yourself to be beautiful, it will shine through and others will see you as beautiful too."

-Elizabeth Paul, 25.

# BLACK & BEAUTIFUL

It saddens me to think about the amount of beautiful black girls who want to change their natural beauty to look less black. They may not do it intentionally. They probably just want to follow what's in-style, but very often that results in white washing our aesthetic. All the while they're aspiring to look like us! Other races of women try to emulate our style, our features, our figures and basically copy our culture yet so many of us still feel ugly and undesirable.

I wake up in the morning everyday feeling beautiful in my brown skin and I believe every other black woman should feel the same. But in this society, it's easier said than done. I didn't always feel secure in my beauty. It's been a journey. Even though my mom and dad called me beautiful and gorgeous as if those were my given names as a little girl, and even though I'd constantly hear it from friends, family and strangers, it's not enough. I looked in the mirror and knew I was beautiful just as I knew that planet earth revolves around the sun, because that's what had been imbedded in my brain.

But I didn't always feel beautiful and there's a big difference.

The media plays a role in raising children, and raising adults even, in a way that people downplay and ignore. It can really eat away at your self-esteem and confidence if you are not armed with an understanding of marketing and advertising. Everyone telling me that I'm beautiful never gave me the confidence as you may think.

Growing up, I wanted to be a model and an actress. Honestly, to this day I beat myself up thinking about this. Chadwick Boseman was my theater teacher in 10th grade at The Urban Assembly School for Music and Art. He's the man who played Jackie Robinson in "42" and James Brown in "Get On Up", which became one of my favorites as he did an amazing job channeling the King of Soul. When I was in high school, he was getting very small roles in pursuit of stardom. I remember working with him one on one with a scene that I wrote. He was impressed by my reading of it and asked me, "so Keisha, you're really good! Do you want to become an actor for real!?" I responded so modestly and said, "Oh no, I just want to do this for fun, I don't think that's realistic."

He looked disappointed but said that he understood my point of view. But in retrospect, I had some nerve telling my teacher, a working actor, that it's not a realistic career. Thank God he didn't listen to me because he got his big break a few years later. I didn't have the confidence to tell my own teacher that I was interested in acting for real.

I pursued modeling in high school. I had professional photo shoots to help me book jobs and nothing much really came of it. As a teen I'd see girls with a certain look getting the most praise and recognition. If it wasn't a white girl, people always wanted to see the biracial girl or the racially ambiguous girl. They were the leads and they were the stars. She might have had a black best friend but at times it was really discouraging. I have a fair skinned mom and a dark-skinned father. I used to wish I would have come out lighter like my mom because maybe then someone would see my star potential. I became more confident and truly felt beautiful for the first time in my life when I embarked on my loc journey, which I will discuss further on.

In the 1990's there was an abundance of black sitcoms that showcased black girls of all shades but once the popularity of sitcoms dropped, I saw less and less black girls on television outside of reality TV. Now more scripted shows are airing, as more and more people are getting over the not-so-real reality shows. I'm so happy that more brown skinned women are getting opportunities in show business. Young black girls are growing up today with far more representation of their own on television. Viola Davis, Issa Rae, Taraji P. Henson,

Kerry Washington and Gabrielle Union are making history and it is a beautiful thing.

"Minority women have a huge problem with self-love and although no reason is the same, it needs to become important for us to learn how to properly care for ourselves. Instead, we try to look for it in the first guy that buys us dinner and a movie.

My experiences with love have taught me the value in taking care of myself and making sure that I'm the best me that I can be. It's okay to be single; God didn't create us just to cook, clean and bear children. We have so much to give in this world and we've come far enough to see that life is still great for those that choose to chase their career and find themselves in whatever it is they love to do.

Understand that not everyone is placed into your life to be your biggest cheerleader, some people are meant to solely teach you lessons and implement growth. God has already preordained steps in our lives and our job is to stay steadfast along that journey. I stopped complaining about all of my trials and tribulations because I began to realize that life is a gift and this gift has purpose.

Forgive the people that do wrong by you and continue to push for better in yourself. And if no one told you today, keep up that confidence girl, it's sexy."

-Monet Collins, 26

@m.c._squared

# REFLECTIONS OF OURSELVES

This is a call for the understanding of self and for recognition of greatness. Not for external validation but for my fellow black women to validate our-selves. For us to realize that it is not our faults. We hold onto a lot of guilt and pain for things that are beyond our doing.

Black woman, if you are reading this, please know that you do not deserve the pain and suffering you have endured. Please, do not have animosity towards your mothers for not being able to teach you the things that she did not even know herself, since her mother was unable and underequipped to teach her either. Like how to feel beautiful in the absence of male reminders or how to distinguish between real love from a king and false love from a jester.

Please, black woman, do not hate your fathers for leaving and not being able to protect you. His father may have left, was incarcerated, murdered, etc. so he never learned how to stay, so the only thing he could have done was leave. He couldn't protect you from the abuser because nobody taught him that was his role as a father. Some fathers are present and leave you with a bad after taste, having you feel like you may have been better off without him around at all. Most people can make children, that is something that happens within us biologically, but that doesn't mean most people will make great parents.

Most of the issues we have with love stem from our parental upbringing. When parents don't encourage, compliment and comfort their children, the child will grow up with issues of self-love and even issues on how to love another. Most of us, men and women, have "mommy issues" or "daddy issues" and those issues are often reflected in how we love ourselves, our partners, other loved ones and even strangers. I think that it is vital that we confront our parents about the issues that we have with them from our childhood, as adults. A conversation could potentially give you a better understanding of them and why things happened the way they did, or you could learn to accept the apology you never received.

Perhaps seeing dysfunction in my parents' marriage and dealing with the absence of my father (who lived only 10 minutes away for many years after their breakup) made me generally avoid dating growing up. In college, as I began dating with a late start in comparison to most of my peers, thoughts of my father and the things he'd done rang constantly in my brain. I had the most disturbing nightmares of being on dates with someone that I had feelings for. Throughout the dreams, my date's face would become my dad's face and I would be confused about who I was having drinks or watching a movie with, my date or my dad? Needless to say, it was very creepy.

When it came to the point that I was having these dreams multiple times a week, I thought I was losing my mind. I visited a counselor on campus after my mother encouraged me to do so when I complained to her about stress. I found the session to be useless. She listened to me rant for 45 minutes and as the time wrapped up, she said I may be depressed and she could schedule an evaluation for me so that I could get medicated. I was incredibly disappointed that medication was the only thing she could offer me. The pharmaceutical industry is very flawed, if you ask me.

I let her schedule the appointment but I never went. Instead, I decided to confront my father about the things I witnessed him do as a child. This was his opportunity to apologize for his actions and provide me with closure, but instead, he chose to deny everything. He said that he never did any of the things I saw him do and that he never would. Here's the kicker, he said I must have dreamed up all of those memories. Mind you, I was not a baby or even a toddler. I was probably a whole entire 10 years old when I saw what I saw! I even recalled him saying, about a year after the instances, that he was trying to forget what happened. I was so insulted that he chose that route, the route of a coward. I told him that he was lying and that I no longer wanted him in my life and he said okay. I was very hurt, stopped speaking to him for about a year. Once I learned to accept him for who he is, I lowered my expectations of him so I was no longer able to be hurt by him. Instead, I felt sympathetic for him.

His biological father passed away before he was born of alcoholism. I'm not entirely sure what his personal relationship was like with his stepfather who passed away when I was 8, but I am sure that people do what they are capable of and nothing more. I believe my dad did his best with the tools he had and I am learning to be at peace with that.

Black women, and black men too, let us never forget the struggles each other has faced. None of us have had an easy ride. **Let's love our black men and women as the reflections of ourselves that we are**. Of course, this means we must first love ourselves to adequately love another.

"Self-love is saying yes to yourself when you want it, but more importantly when you need it. Self-love is, or should be, shameless thoughts or acts reinforcing that regardless, despite, or in addition to the love you receive. You are deserving of love from the person who matters most – yourself."

-Dominique Harrison, 25

# SELF-LOVE IS...

Do you know what it means to love yourself? Loving yourself can mean different things for different people. We all have to find out what self-love means to us as individuals. To discover what it takes to love yourself, you must learn yourself and discover your passions. The process will involve plenty trial and error. Mistakes will be made. It may come with tears and heartache but that's all in the process. You can't truly learn what it is you need without learning what you don't need.

Learning yourself also takes a lot of courage. It can be scary to confront yourself fully and truthfully. It can be frightening to face your inner you because we build walls to block vulnerability to avoid emotional pain. This behavior won't serve us, it'll block our blessings and stunt our growth as a spiritual being in our human experience. We have to be courageous enough to open ourselves up to ourselves, confront our own triggers head on and rediscover who we truly are and who we may be suppressing in order to learn how to love ourselves.

For me personally, self-love is about maintaining my wellness and prioritizing my mental health.

Self-love is waking up in the morning and thanking God for my many blessings and showing the world that I am grateful for all the good things I have.

Self-love is also being appreciative for all the bad things I've experienced because it helps me to be gracious even more so for the good and teaches valuable lessons.

Self-love is believing that my aspirations are tangible and doing everything in my power to actualize them.

Self-love is showing interest in my appearance, putting time and energy into my presentation as well as being confident in myself even when I am looking a mess.

Self-love is spending time with my loved ones, being honest and open with them when I feel hurt by them and by being apologetic when I hurt them as well.

Self-love is disconnecting from social media and turning my phone off for some peaceful time in solitude when I need it.

Self-love is increasing my water intake and actively incorporating more raw and live fruits and vegetables in my diet.

Self-love is knowing when to say no to others and when to say yes to myself.

Self-love is playing "FUBU" by Solange Knowles on repeat at the highest volume, singing along.

Self-love is getting myself away from negative situations, quitting bad and unhealthy habits, acknowledging that I may be on different frequencies than others and there is no need to force friendships and relationships into working or lasting if they don't serve me and make me better.

Self-love can be many things to different people, once you learn what it takes to love yourself, do it and watch how much your life will change. It is vital to actively work towards loving yourself. Do it for the upliftment of our children. Do it for your spiritual growth and ascension. Do it for the sake of the world we live in. When you love yourself, it becomes so easy to love another. We'll become more in tune with our own needs and the needs of others so that we can help each other live in harmony. I just solved the world's problems. You're welcome.

If only it were that simple. Beginning to truly love yourself is far easier said than done. It takes a lot of consideration, effort and dedication. It can be done on your own but it's always great to have a support system, someone who knows you've embarked on a self-love journey, who understands its importance and is possibly going on the same journey as you as well.

Does this make you selfish? Dedicating all this time and energy into yourself when there are so many people who are in need? So many people who are depending on you? Absolutely not. How can you effectively help anyone else when you haven't been helped yourself. You shouldn't feed anyone when you, yourself have yet to be fed.

Remember, you were once an infant. You weren't raised by another infant. You were raised by relatively grown individuals who had the tools to help you grow. Once you have grown, you then can do the same for an infant. You owe it to the village who raised you to become the best version of you as you can be. You are an investment. Everyone involved in your growth, your parents, family members, religious leaders, teachers, professors, etc. all played a major role in shaping you into you. They've invested time, money and energy into your development. Yes, often they make mistakes, fall short and disappoint but you are a product of love.

One way to show the same love back to all of the influential people in your life is by loving you, too. If you can't find the desire or motivation to love yourself for any other reason, do it for the ones who love you.

"Self-love is a tricky little thing! It's like the rose that grows out of concrete. I find that the women that value themselves the most are the ones that have had to learn to do so the hard way. And even when you get to a place where you're comfortable with yourself and have accepted your flaws… bam, the universe knocks right on that door with a new lesson to learn!

You never love yourself "enough", the party's never done. Since we never stop growing, we're constantly learning and having to accept the ever-changing facets of ourselves. It's funny because we worship the people in our lives that put up with our bull… but putting up with your own bull as you fall and get up and try again is the greatest feat! I find that beautiful.

Sticking with yourself through the flaws, through the mistakes and through the hard lessons is so beautiful. Finding the worthiness in that journey is the true definition self-love."

-Ieasha Tiffany, 25. @ieashatiffany

"In the matter of love, we must first love internally in order to manifest the full force of our love externally. There is no shame in loving yourself or who you aspire to be. Shame comes from not accepting and believing in who you are meant to be."

-Mandy Mc., 30. @lipstk_n_locs

# SELF-LOVE IN QUESTION

It isn't always easy to recognize behaviors indicative of lacking self-love, especially if you haven't established standards for yourself. So many of us are quick to create lists of what our "dream man" should be. 'He must be a Renaissance man with financial freedom, opens doors, over 6' tall, sends good morning texts, has perfect hygiene with a large…' How can we create standards for our lover without meeting standards for ourselves or even creating them to begin with? This is when learning and knowing ourselves is vital. Once we are able to learn ourselves, we can set standards for ourselves to abide by and love ourselves accordingly. Sometimes it takes trauma for us to be able to identify what it is we need for ourselves and from our lover.

I graduated from SUNY Albany in 2013 with a BA in Africana Studies and Sociology. Fortunately for me, when I went to college my mother was very lenient about what I chose to study because she wanted to make sure I was interested in what I was learning so that I did well and earned high grades. I graduated with a good GPA but my BA wasn't very attractive to employers. It appeared that most of my peers went straight on to earn a Master's degree, knowing a BA in Africana Studies wouldn't hold much weight in the workforce.

Needless to say, I struggled finding work that put my degree to use so I ended up working several different temporary and part time jobs my first two years out of school. I even started selling loc jewelry online and monetized my YouTube videos to earn more income. I worked meaningful jobs, working with homeless children and helping at-risk youth get ready for college but it wasn't enough to satisfy me; I felt that I needed to work a 9-5 to feel like a real adult. I finally scored my first full time job in 2015 at a facility for people with mental illness.

I loved my job, at first. I worked at an organization that helps high functioning people with mental illness get jobs, housing, any and everything they need. I especially loved working there because it opened my eyes to the fact that mental illness does not discriminate. I worked closely with people who had PhDs and were home owners as well as people who were homeless with middle school level education, all with severe mental illness. I learned a lot and did my job very well, however I felt stuck. There wasn't much room for growth without higher degrees and I didn't know if I wanted to stay in the field of mental health. I was confused; I didn't know if I should stay or go but I chose to stay because I got comfortable there.

Ever since I was a teenager I had extremely painful periods, more painful than most of my friends. I tried birth control and prescription pain relievers but nothing helped long term. The longer I worked at my full time job, the more painful my periods were. The cramping became debilitating and I started getting migraines. Before long, I managed to max out all my paid time off, vacation time, personal time, all of it. I didn't understand why I was suddenly experiencing so much pain. The only thing different in my life was my job.

I started to get depressed. I couldn't identify what was wrong with me. I was earning what was a decent income at the time and I could do what I really loved on the side, which was create YouTube videos and craft my handmade accessories. I thought it was time to seek help from a professional to discover what was truly troubling me.

After one quick google search I found a holistic therapist. For some reason, the black community frowns upon seeking therapy. Perhaps because we believe we are too strong and don't need it or because *all we need is Jesus*. Either way, I chose to remain open-minded, especially since the therapist was holistic and I knew she wouldn't try to prescribe me any medications like the counselor in Albany tried to recommend.

I visited the therapist a few times. I felt incredibly awkward expressing myself to a stranger but a large part of me was desperate to 'fix' whatever was wrong with me. She kept asking me questions about my early childhood that I could not easily answer.

My early memories are incredibly vague, as are most people's memories, I assumed. She tried several different activities to try to get me to relive my early childhood and she concluded that my memories were suppressed and I possibly experienced trauma as a young child. At that point I decided to no longer visit her. I wasn't paying her to discuss my childhood, I didn't think that would help me discover why I suddenly felt so depressed today. I still decided to keep her words in mind so I did some of the activities she showed me regularly.

In March 2016, I experienced one of the scariest and most painful experiences of my life. I hit an all-time low and couldn't get out of bed for days as a result. There was no way I could advise a single person on my case load with my own mental health on the line. I quit my job. I felt like a failure in all aspects of my life. Once I decided to stop feeling sorry for myself, I started to listen to lectures on YouTube to help pick myself up. Among the hundreds of videos I watched, I came across a couple questions that were asked multiple times: "Who was the parent whose love you craved the most? How did you try to get their love when it wasn't given?"

I recalled taking Psych 101 my freshman year in college and often it was emphasized how much early childhood experiences, from birth to about age 5, played a role in who you become as a person. Experiences that we take for granted play a major role in the person we grow up to be. Did our parents hug and kiss us often? Lack of emotional support can lead to temperamental issues in the child well into adulthood. Did we witness our parents arguing regularly? Such behavior normalizes negative communication between man and woman especially in relationships.

I thought it would be beneficial to give the question serious thought and I had an epiphany. Though my parents were married until I was about 15 years old, my dad was out of my home by the age 11. Although I have photos being held and kissed by my father as a child, I could barely recall actual memories of myself receiving affection from my father. I remember him being very silly at times but mostly militant towards my siblings and me. He was in the Air Force. After my parents broke up, I initiated contact most of the time. He always was first to say 'I love you' and he would repeat it multiple times as if he was trying to convince me that it was true.

I didn't take things personally because I knew he is an alcoholic; my mom taught me that alcoholism is a disease so I felt like he couldn't help that he didn't truly love me. I accepted whatever he believed to be love and I was doomed to subconsciously accept whatever kind of love I would receive from men because of him, with feelings of never being worthy of the love I desired.

I would visit my father from time to time and he would always focus the conversation around what he was up to, rarely asking about my life. When I volunteered information about what was going on with me, he wouldn't show much interest as he never asked follow up questions to show that he was even listening. I became very good at just chalking up all of his shortcomings to the fact that he is an alcoholic and I was content with that, so I thought. But perhaps my father's disdain led me to believe that I was never enough. If I was never enough for my father to commit to quitting drinking, I thought I may never be enough for a man to commit to loving. I found myself settling in different aspects of my life, including my job as a mental health worker.

I broke my own heart settling so much. My emotional pain manifested into physical pain through my worsening menstrual cycle and migraines. This period of my life was perhaps the time my self-love was in question the most.

"We grow through life. We don't always make the best choices when we're younger. But when we know better, we do better."

-Jenelle Nurse, 32

# GROWTH FROM FAILURE

Since I was a child I wanted to impress my parents with accomplishments, whether academic or extracurricular, I always wanted to make sure that I was exemplary. Throughout my many accomplishments over the years, I rarely felt celebrated. Perhaps my loved ones simply expected me to do well to the point that they probably felt that my accomplishments did not need to be acknowledged.

At the Queen Series event in 2014, I was a guest speaker. In my speech I emphasized the importance of not drawing your confidence from your appearance. Society exalts a Eurocentric standard of beauty that black women should not subscribe to or else it would eat away at a black woman's self-esteem. I emphasized that instead, we should draw our confidence from our achievements such as degrees, awards and promotions but now I feel like I couldn't have been more wrong. Of course, we shouldn't draw all of our confidence in looks, even if we do fit society's standards, because looks are fleeting. But getting our confidence from rewards can mean we are in constant need of other people's approval.

I tried to follow that way of thinking throughout my life and I realize now that it creates a temporary sense of satisfaction but soon that feeling fades away. The feeling often morphs into discontent because the accolades dwindle or aren't what was expected. Trying to prove yourself as worthy can be one of the most draining things you can do. Whether trying to show a mate that you are worthy of their love or trying to show a crowd that you are worthy of ovation, putting your self-esteem in another's control is incredibly dangerous. You are handing over your power.

Confidence should never come from external sources. If other people are in control of your confidence you can never be too secure because people are fickle. It's funny how love can turn to hate when you disagree with a popular opinion or if you are deemed as no longer beneficial or useful. Rather than getting your sense of confidence from accomplishments that other people reward you, draw your confidence from within and most of all, progression.

We often work very hard, set goals and fail. Whether the failure was in the form of a relationship that didn't end well or even a poor investment that went south, we let that failure eat away at our confidence. Failures diminish self-esteem because of wrong perspectives.

Rather than dwelling on the defeat, focus on the lesson to foster growth. If you are unable to find a lesson from unfortunate circumstances, then you truly fail. But if you can acknowledge your perseverance and recognize your progress then you can never fail. That is something we all can draw confidence from.

"We make self-love seem like this complicated concept. It's really about being comfortable in your own skin. It doesn't mean you don't have flaws or insecurities, it only means that you're self-aware and can handle the idea of being imperfect. And while the opinions of others matter more than we'd like to admit, our perception of ourselves ultimately guide the opinions of others.

March to the beat of your own drum. The more you listen to it, the more you'll enjoy it. The more you enjoy it, the more others will too. Make it a song that people can't get out of their heads."

-Rii Fitzgerald-Fields, 42. @missrii

# HOW TO SELF-LOVE

Everyone knows that the first step towards solving a problem is accepting that there is one. Most of us, when asked if we love ourselves, will say yes. Automatically. Without a moment of thought or consideration. But I ask you to truly take a moment to consider what self-love means to you. Now tell me, do you love yourself? Maybe you do, and if you do, I am happy for you but if you're still here on Earth in this human form then there is still room left for growth. For the others, maybe you don't love yourself very much. If you don't, I hope I can help you make some progress by the end of this read.

We often look outside of ourselves for happiness, for security, for love. That is where we go wrong. Can you bare your own thoughts? Can you stand being alone? Do you always feel the need to be in a relationship? Do you constantly need to feel another temporary rush or high, whether substance induced or not? Do you take part in very risky behavior, constantly putting your life on the line? These are some things you may want to consider when gauging your self-love.

Remember that feeling confident and loving yourself isn't some elusive dream you had during a nap on a Sunday afternoon. It isn't a fantasy novel you read for an 8th grade book report either. There is nothing truer than love. It is very possible to love yourself unconditionally and once your mind is at the destination of confidence and self-love, your life can follow the path.

Accepting yourself fully and wholeheartedly will guide you in the right direction. We are all flawed. Our flaws don't make us bad people but they make us individuals. Unfortunately, it's second nature to gauge our self-worth in relation to the value we place on other people. We decide people are worthy because of their physical characteristics like brawn and beauty. We also give them value based on their accomplishments and possessions like degrees and income. Then we compare ourselves to others and decide how much love we deserve. Is this natural?

What do you have to offer the world, another individual or even just yourself? If you cannot think of anything, I invite you to embark on a new journey and accept this challenge.

Create a list of things that scare you. Include the places you are afraid to go and the things you are afraid to try, like sky diving. Create another list, something like your bucket list (you know, the things you want to do before you *kick the bucket*). This list should comprise of the exciting things that you want to do, but never got around to, like taking a mixed martial arts class. Lastly, create a third list. This list will consist of your goals. Fill this list up with your dreams and aspirations, things you have always wanted to accomplish like finishing that second master's degree.

Now that you have these lists, hang them on your wall somewhere you will see every single day. Read them daily. Constantly seeing them every day will make it far more likely that you will face your fears, take leaps of faith and get them done. Setting goals and accomplishing them is a sure-fire way to enhance your sense of self-love and confidence.

"Love is unexplainable. True love is indescribable. You'll know when it happens. When it happens you will eat, sleep, breathe that person. You will dream that person. But instead of having nightmares like dreams you had of your ex, these dreams you won't want to wake up from. Love doesn't hurt. It's not painful. You both will make mistakes but those mistakes shouldn't happen over and over and disappointment shouldn't be a routine.

And ladies, it's okay to say no. Let losers stay single. Those 'I don't work, I hustle' losers. Those 'can I drop you off at work and use your car for the day and pick you up late' losers. I've been there. It's draining. You think your favors will make him love you more. He doesn't love you more. He barely loves you at all. Until he loves himself he can never love you like you deserve. Don't be afraid to grow. Grow together or grow apart, but grow. Reading this book is a step in the right direction. God bless."

-Monique Collins, 26

# BALANCE

This may not always be realistic and I am still trying to figure out if this is ideal, but at this stage in my life and self-love journey, I believe maintaining an emotional balance is an essential skill to cultivate. I tend to get overzealous and excited when certain events occur that bring me joy. On the converse side of things, I tend to get very dejected and miserable during hard times. I believe people will be better off if they can maintain a steady inner climate of serenity. This can be maintained by living in the moment more, without overthinking.

Refraining from dwelling on the past and worrying about the future can encourage inner peace. Half of our sadness and stress come from things that already happened, that we have no influence over since we cannot change the past. The other half of our sadness and stress come from our fears and uncertainties of the future since we cannot predict what is to come. **All we can do is our best with what we have today, to heighten our chances of a better tomorrow.** Staying in the moment will lessen the chances of being stuck in a miserable state.

Staying in motion is very helpful to keep a healthy state of mind. You should never do too much or work too hard to distract yourself from your life, but having a full schedule with adequate 'me time' will help out in the bad times.

Checking in with yourself from time to time to assess your feelings and emotions can be a great help. Being aware of your emotions is important so that you can understand your triggers and take the necessary steps to fix your state of mind. It will also help to communicate these feelings to your loved ones so that they understand you more. It'll help prevent you from displacing your anger to them or if you do, they won't take it personally.

Remaining grateful for what you have and giving selflessly to those less fortunate is essential for keeping a balanced state of mind. Remembering where you came from to get to where you are and helping those in positions where you once were will keep you grounded and humble. So many people change and become 'hollywood' once they get a taste of success because they are so excited to finally make it out of whatever circumstance they are coming from. But these are the people who tend to fall down the hardest once they run out of gas.

Remaining humble and keeping an emotional balance has always been important to me. I can recall an instance in my life when I had one of my highest highs and lowest lows within the span of a couple hours and it taught me the importance of having a balance for my emotional health.

I was about 15 years old when I got selected to model for my first talent agency. I was so excited because I believed I finally got my foot in the door. I was going to be the next Tyra Banks. At the time, I had a healthy obsession with her. I would rush home from school to catch her talk show and I would watch America's Next Top Model religiously taking mental notes. I was on cloud nine! My mother and I signed the paperwork, scheduled my first photoshoot for the following week and headed home.

At the time, we were living on the edge of East Flatbush, Brooklyn towards Brownsville so the Saratoga stop on the 3 train was closest to home. I talked my mother's ear off the whole ride home from Downtown Manhattan, about how excited I was, how grateful I was that she agreed to let me pursue my dreams, and how eager I was to get started booking shoots, shows and commercials.

We got home early in the evening. My brother was about 17 and had been at track practice and he was expected to be home already. My grandparents were home though, and my mother figured that my brother was just hanging out after practice and forgot to call. I signed onto the internet to instant message my friends to let them know of the big moves I'd be making soon. We weren't home for a full 10 minutes when my mother's cellphone rang and it was my brother's number.

"J.R? …Yes, this is his mother… Oh God! Oh God!" I could only hear my mom's side of the conversation but I knew something terrible must have happened.

"Keisha, let's go to Saratoga. J.R's been stabbed on the 3 train."

"Is he okay?"

"I don't know, an MTA worker just called. Let's go."

My grandparents insisted on coming with us so my mother walked slowly with them. I didn't have the patience to walk with them and my mother wanted an update as soon as possible so I went ahead.

I decided to call my dad. I hadn't spoken to him in a few months at the time but I figured he'd care to know his only son had been stabbed. I wondered if my brother would have wanted him to know, and I concluded that he probably would rather that I didn't tell him. Something told me to just call him anyway, so I did.

"Hey, dad."

"Hey, baby."

"Umm, I thought I should let you know J.R got stabbed. I don't have any details but he's at the train so I'm going to see him now."

"What!?"

"J.R got stabbed."

"No, no, no, no, no." I had never heard my father get emotional before unless he was drunk but this time he sounded very clear and sober.

"What hospital is he going to?"

"I didn't get any information yet, I am on my way to the train to see him and find out. But it's safe to say Brookdale Hospital since it's so close."

"Okay, I'm going to meet you all at the hospital," he said and we got off the phone.

It's usually a 10-minute walk but this time around I made it in 5. In retrospect, I don't know why my mom didn't drive. We all would have made it in 2 minutes. But perhaps my mom didn't want to deal with taking the car out of the gate.

I saw a bunch of seemingly lost teenagers and figured they must have been his track team members from Brooklyn Tech High School. I approached the ambulance and saw my brother. He was sitting up and appeared fine until he shouted hello to me. I could tell that he had trouble breathing as it took a lot out of him to shout. A few minutes later, my mother and grandparents arrived.

Apparently, some kid tried to steal his friend's iPod on the train. My brother got in a fight with the guy in her defense. He got stabbed in the fight but didn't realize it due to the adrenaline rush he had. After he got off the train he collapsed and that's when he knew he had gotten seriously hurt. He was stabbed in his left lung.

My father called me to let me know he had arrived at the hospital. The ambulance hadn't even taken off yet. What was taking them so long? This is an emergency, didn't they have any sense of urgency!? I was shocked my dad arrived so quickly since he lived on the other side of East Flatbush, closer to Kings County Hospital. Before the ambulance took off, J.R shouted to me and his teammates to let us know he's okay. My mother promptly told him to stop since he already had issues breathing. At this point he didn't know his lung was punctured.

When the ambulance finally took off, it went the wrong way. Not only did the ambulance take forever to take off, but it went in the wrong direction when it finally does!? I didn't like whatever game they were playing. My brother could have gotten to Brookdale Hospital sooner if I carried him on my back myself! I'm not even exaggerating. The hospital was just a couple minutes away on Rockaway Parkway and Linden Blvd. That's just about 5 long blocks from the train station.

I walked my grandparents back home and told myself I'd walk over to the hospital to be with my mother, father and brother. Once my grandparents were settled, I walked to the hospital and was stuck in my thoughts. Just over an hour earlier I had gotten the best news of my life and in an instant I got the worst. My brother endured a life-threatening attack to his lung. They told him if he wasn't in such good shape, he could have died. I was overcome with emotions once I reached the hospital, so much so that I turned around and went back home. The automatic doors opened for me but I couldn't even bring myself inside.

You are guaranteed to have highs and lows in life and if you live enough, you'll have your highs and lows in the same day like I did. Finding your balance is the way to fight the funk and push through.

"Do you remember the first time you felt sad? I don't. We always focus on the bad of the moment and feel like that pain can never go away. The biggest lesson in life is that it will be okay. I don't remember the pain from years back because I moved on. The endless possibilities we have in the future sometimes is crippled by the past. So in the moment of weakness, sorrow, pain and suffering, just know it won't last long. It will only last the longer you hold onto it."

-Kimberley Smith, 25.

# FROM REJECTION TO OBSESSION

As a huge Beyonce fan that I am, I admittedly listen to her music without considering the lyrics and what message it may be conveying. In the summer of 2010, Beyonce's music video for her song "Why Don't You Love Me?" was released on YouTube and I played it repeatedly. I was captivated by the quick, danceable tempo, the vintage imagery in the music video and of course Beyonce's incredible vocals and beauty.

In the song, Beyonce lists all the areas in which she thrives and is questioning why her man doesn't love her. She claims she's easy to love because she's beautiful, classy, stylish and sexy. She points out that she's financially independent, smart, and a freak in the sheets. In the video, Beyonce is taking on the role of a homemaker, watering the plants, cleaning the house, cooking dinner, attempting to fix the car's engine, doing laundry and even bathing all while maintaining her sex appeal. When she can't figure out why he doesn't love her, she simply concludes that "he's just plain dumb."

"Keisha, why do you keep playing that song?" My sister, Jenelle, asked me with a slight air of disgust.

I replied without much thought, "I don't know, I just like it." Her response shocked me and led me to seriously analyze the problematic lyrics.

"How pathetic does a woman have to be, to feel the need to explain why she's worthy of being loved to a man? He doesn't want her and he doesn't have to."

My sister has the tendency to randomly overanalyze song lyrics but I felt like this time she was spot on. We women are often overly concerned with why a certain man isn't interested in us and why he chose another woman instead. When will we become more concerned with why we are so interested in this certain man who refuses to give us the love we believe we deserve?

Instead of moving on to love ourselves and find a man who can love us right, we try so hard to become the ideal woman that we believe men want us to be. We are quick to call ourselves "wife material". What is "wife material", anyway? Is it a fabric? Is it sold by the yard? I wonder if it's silky...

It is naive to believe that all men are the same and that they all require the same type of woman. If so many women claim to be good women who are cut from the same wife cloth, what makes you any different? What would make a man want to choose you over another woman? That goes to show that taking care of "wifely duties," is not enough to make a man fall in love with you, there are tons of women who can cook, clean and are great in bed, so being skilled in those areas doesn't make you special. What is it about you as a person that makes you special?

Now, I am not saying that Beyonce is problematic for performing this song. The song is very expressive of the feelings many woman have when they feel rejected by a man that they think they love, especially when they believe they proved themselves worthy. Often, we women actually do love these men, but I believe women are quick to call something love when it's just lust or infatuation.

People want to fall in love but falling has never been a pleasant experience, I would much rather grow in love. Some of us are so desperate to love someone and to feel loved by another that we choose to love someone before they have shown different sides to their personality, how they act in different situations around different people and before they show you that they are emotionally available, ready and worthy to be loved by you.

The way a person behaves when they are rejected by the opposite sex is a huge indicator of their self-love status. Someone with healthy levels of self-love may take the rejection in stride. They may believe that it wasn't personal. Maybe it was bad timing or it wasn't a right fit. Someone lacking self-love may begin to obsess over several things like their body image or their facial features, the rejecter himself or even the women that the rejecter has dated or is interested in.

Women trying so hard to change their character for the sole reason of getting a husband usually end up miserable in the long run because they are suppressing their true selves. You can always get your dream man by being the woman he wants but how will you sustain the relationship over time? Rather than being the woman you think a man wants, become the greatest version of yourself so you will naturally attract the best man for you.

Good men are constantly questioning why do good girls go for bad boys? These men get played and overlooked on a regular basis and often decide to act like the bad boys who do get the girl. Ignore your calls, text you back sometimes and make empty promises because they sound good at the moment. Now they get the attention that they weren't getting when they were sweet, caring and considerate. So many women claim they want good men but get addicted to bad boys.

Do women like to be treated badly? No, we don't. We want to be loved and appreciated but we often get enticed by the thrill of chasing a man who isn't showing as much interest in us, as we do in them. It's a lot like the high people get from gambling. It is human nature to be attracted to the thrill of the risk over the end result which often isn't as gratifying. Women, when thinking logically know bad boys aren't their ideal man but still try to win them over much like placing a risky bet. The reward of getting the guy isn't as satisfying as the rush you feel when dealing with the uncertainty.

Depending on the woman, one or two heartbreaks from a bad boy type will teach them that the end result isn't worth the risk. The naive woman lacking self-love will continue to play these dangerous games but the mature woman who loves herself enough will not accept such inconsistency from a man who claims to have her best interest at heart.

"Every day you're faced with a challenge, but always know *this too shall pass.*"

-Brittany Lingard, 25.

@_brittstagram


"Love is supposed to last for eternity… but eternity doesn't last forever. Love has no expiration date. It is the people that we choose to let expire."

-Tyree V, 26.

# END OF A RELATIONSHIP IS NOT A FAILURE

Consider the fact that most romantic relationships come to an end but most people don't enter a relationship anticipating its ending. Anybody who does, honestly, truly, has no business getting into a relationship in the first place, but I digress. We often see ourselves as great disappointments when our relationships end. Understandably so, since we women typically get into relationships with hopes of our man being 'the one,' and we try to make it work long after our gut tells us it's through. We try to force a square peg in a circle hole because we don't want the time and energy we invested into the relationship to be in vain. We don't want the next woman to benefit from our hard work and we want to maintain an image to our friends, family and general public as if we have something to prove.

When we finally accept that for whatever reason the relationship must come to an end, or even if our lover is the one who decides to end things, it can crush our entire world. I'm sure most people can relate to that empty feeling after a breakup. You have great news, like a promotion at work or you bumped into an old mutual friend you hadn't seen in ages. You want to tell them all about it but then you remember, it's over. Random things in your home they purchased for you, certain songs or movies remind you of times you've shared. It can all be very painful. Pain comes from resistance of truth. Once we are able to accept the truth of the matter, we can move on and move forward.

We would experience far less pain after a breakup if we would stop viewing the ended relationship as a failure. **The perspectives that you choose in life will always shape your experiences, good or bad.** Try a different perspective. Recognize that the relationship was an opportunity for you to learn more about yourself, in ways that you couldn't have learned on your own or with someone else.

A relationship is a success if it is able to show you some of your flaws that you didn't know existed. It is a success if you were able to get a better understanding of what you want and need from your partner in a relationship so that you can communicate it to your future lover. A relationship is a success if you were able to learn from mistakes you made so that you don't repeat them in your next relationship. Whether you stay together or go your separate ways, a relationship can be a success if you acknowledge the things that you are walking away with; a greater sense of self.

"When I truly start to silence the voices and believe in me, life becomes a little easier. Smiles are more frequent and joy becomes abundant."

-Shana Boatswain, 32. @essenceofshay

# MORE THAN A HAIR JOURNEY

As black women, going on a natural hair journey or a loc journey is a major tool that will guide you in the direction of self-love and confidence. Such a journey helps you to see yourself as if it were for the first time. Many black women choose to wear fake hair to feel beautiful. The women whose hair we wear resemble the hair of women that are exalted all over the world. These women are viewed as the most cherished and accepted as beautiful and desirable. We are taught that our own hair is wrong and needs to be fixed or changed to conform and be the type of beauty that society embraces. So we permanently straighten our hair and wear wigs and/or weaves covering our natural hair.

When I first started my locs it was summer break. I was home from my first year away at college and wasn't around friends as often as I had been during the school year. I battled with myself, feeling like I looked less than a woman with my short little coils. I felt insecure without my crutch in the form of long box braids, my transition style.

In High School I had long relaxed hair. I barely even knew what my natural texture was like since I got my roots touched-up every 6 weeks. I gradually cut my perm off and wore braid extensions for ten months to grow my natural hair for locs. Ten months was adequate time to grow my hair long enough to get long starter locs, right? Wrong. My coils were only about two-three inches after shrinkage. When I first looked at myself in the mirror, I wasn't as pleased as I would have liked to be yet I was happy that my journey had begun.

As the days, weeks and months went by I started to accept myself more and more unapologetically. Facing myself with my guard down I realized this was me. I am who I am and I need no excuses.

I didn't go through a breakup nor was I having a mental breakdown. I just wanted to be me and I needed to learn who that is. I wanted to feel beautiful in my own skin and I didn't need long straight hair for that anymore. On my own and in public, I wore my hair out proudly. I wore a headwrap around my home-friends so that my hair wouldn't be the subject of conversation all the time. I didn't want to keep explaining and reexplaining my decisions to the friends who were against my choice.

University started back and my security started to diminish. I didn't feel as beautiful as I did at home where I was more comfortable. Most of my peers didn't have locs or even natural hair at all. Most people I encountered refused to comment on my hair as if to spare my feelings. My hair was the elephant in the room. It was a drastic change in my physical appearance yet it was totally ignored. I bought a wig.

"Forgive because it benefits you more than your offender. Forgiving means you've grown to see the faults and maybe positives in that person and how you can live peacefully around them or with them. It doesn't mean allowing them into the same space they violated or abused. It's not a matter of being petty. You're simply protecting your heart and psyche."

-Liz R. 34 @locsmermaidiaa

"Sometimes in life if you're so fortunate, God blesses you with a special treasure called friendship."

-Ruqayyah Batts, 25.

# AARON JOHNSON

I was always the type of girl to have a large clique of friends but I often felt like an outsider in my friend groups. While my friends were interacting in large company, I would prefer to hangout in smaller numbers. I felt that was when people feel more comfortable being themselves. I cherish the bonds that I have with my friends individually. The time I've spent with my closest friends alone and in small groups mean a lot to me. One on one time shared is priceless because that's when I'm able to truly learn who they are since they can speak more freely without worrying about judgment from the group.

He was one of my closest friends in high school. I loved hanging out with him in the group because he was always funny and could uplift anyone effortlessly. However, when we were in the group, I distanced myself from him because I often felt like he was putting on a show. I didn't need to be entertained by him, I just wanted him to be himself. But entertaining the crowd made him feel good so I accepted it. He loved having everyone's attention but I cared more about cultivating my bond with him personally, so we kept our friendship mostly outside of school. We hung out on weekends at his house or his sister's shop and spoke on the phone after school for hours at a time.

When I started college, I was in *a different world*, no pun intended. I wasn't nurturing my high school friendships as much as I'd have liked since my new college life took all my attention. Plus, my friendship with him had been in shambles after I started questioning his loyalty towards the end of my senior year in high school. I knew he betrayed my trust but never addressed him about it. I just ignored his invitations and barely spoke to him. He realized I was purposely distancing myself from him so he did the same.

It was March 7th, 2010. The day after my 19th birthday during my second semester of freshman-year and I hadn't heard from him since September when I called him for his birthday. We probably spoke for 30 seconds. He cut the conversation short after I invited him to visit me in Albany. He was in the middle of socializing with his friends so I didn't take it personal when he rushed me off the phone. But 6 months went by and we hadn't spoken. On this day, March 7th, he shot me a text. I was in the university library working on an assignment but decided to respond and be passive aggressive.

"Hey, Keish. It's Arie, I got a new number."

"Yo…"

"I miss you, Keisha…"

"Yeah, whatever"

"Stop it!"

"You miss me, so you text me the day after my birthday?"

"I'm not good at remembering birthdays, sorry, I forgot."

"It's okay, I'll just forget when September 22nd rolls back around." September 22nd is his birthday. I'm so clever, right?

"Stop, Killa! I know what I did and why you haven't spoken to me. I'm sorry I wasn't a good friend to you. You didn't deserve that."

"Thanks for saying that, I appreciate it."

"Can I call you tomorrow?"

"Okay, Spliff." That was my nickname for him for a period of time back in the day.

"Aww! You're back!"

"Lol"

I was so relieved that we were back speaking. What happened wasn't worth losing our friendship. I wish I had been open with him about my feelings of betrayal when it happened instead of just pushing him to the back burner. We didn't get to speak the next day as we had planned. The day after that, March 9, 2010, I was informed that he was murdered in front of his home in East Flatbush, Brooklyn.

I realize I'm incredibly lucky that I was able to make peace with my friend before his life was taken. However, I do wish that I was mature enough to address my feelings of betrayal to him the moment I felt betrayed. Our fall-out wasn't worth ending our friendship, especially since his days were numbered. We could have discussed what occurred calmly and moved forward.

Holding a grudge does more damage to yourself than it does to anybody else. Your anger at them only hardens your own heart. It doesn't hurt them at all. Sometimes you have to accept the apology you never received. You aren't required to keep the offender in your life but **you have to let go of the hurt and anger and set yourself free**. Have you ever let go of pain and heart ache that you had been holding onto for a long time? I have. I actually felt the energy leave my chest and float on, into the air. Holding onto pain affects you physically, so let it go, be well and breathe deeply.

Aaron died while I was transitioning from relaxed to natural hair. I attended his funeral with my hair in box braids. I started my locs immediately after the semester ended in May. When June rolled around, my friends and I decided to throw a surprise dinner for Aaron's mom at her home, the location of so many parties and gatherings we enjoyed tremendously. Aaron's house was "the spot" so we felt it was appropriate. We collaborated with his sister to pull it off. It was a success, although Mrs. Johnson came home early and caught us preparing. She was very appreciative of our efforts and loved seeing us all again in her house as we used to be there so much when Aaron was alive.

At this point, my baby locs were only a month old and I wore them in a headwrap almost daily. Most people didn't know I was locking my hair unless I told them, especially since I wore headwraps from time to time with my relaxed hair underneath in the past. I told one of Aaron's friends that I cut off my perm to start my locs and she was shocked. Her jaw dropped, she covered her mouth with both hands and opened her eyes wide. I looked at her in her eyes with the straightest face thinking, *girl relax*. I told her I went natural and she looked at me as if she saw a ghost.

> "Aaron always bragged about his friend Keisha with the long hair," she said.
>
> "He knew I wanted to get locs. My hair will get long again," I snapped at her in my defense.
>
> "But anybody can have long hair with locs. Most black girls' hair doesn't grow long like yours with a perm. You should have

embraced that." She explained her perspective with her twisted logic.

She sounded so foolish to me but I knew so many people would have shared her stance. Should I be acknowledged because I managed to be able to retain length despite abusing 'the creamy crack?' I just ignored her statement and moved on from the subject. Sometimes I prefer to build with people who are already on the same page as me. It's far too draining to try to build with someone who's in a different chapter or a completely different book. Perhaps I was being judgmental, figuring that she wouldn't understand my perspective, but I knew we were on completely different stages in our life journeys and that is okay.

"Becoming a mother has made me conscious of how I love myself. I want my daughter to see me healthy, physically and spiritually."

-Tai McLeod, 26.

@taigio

# STYLE, WHAT ARE YOU PROTECTING?

I called my new wig that I wore in Albany, a protective style, which it was. Typically, protective styles are for protecting hair from external factors such as extreme heat, cold, humidity, combs, flat irons, and general manipulation. This wig protected me from my insecurities and self-doubt. It protected me from the sideways stares and the whispers.

People who never commented on my locs started commenting on my wig. "Nice wig, no more locs?" I felt hurt that people seemed happy that I no longer showed my locs. Did they not see my bravery? My strength? My beauty in my natural state? My wig reminded me of why I needed my locs. I don't need a crutch. No filter. No mask. No excuses. No apologies. Locs don't need to be the most popular style for me to love my hair. I don't need any of those things and quite frankly I don't need my locs but they have been an excellent tool to help me accept myself wholly.

In life, we are indirectly taught that a very specific hairstyle is what is acceptable, straight hair. When our hair grows kinky, curly and coily, naturally, that gives us a strong message subconsciously. It can tell us that who we truly are is unacceptable. That is an idea that we, as black people, are taught. People don't come up with the ideas that the way they look is ugly completely on their own.

I believe we are born with self-love but life can slowly drain our sense of self-love without us even realizing. Babies, when adequately nurtured, are incredibly happy. They love to laugh and smile for seemingly no reason at all. The way we raise our kids, and the things we expose them to will encourage or break the happiness they were born with.

I worked at a homeless shelter in South Jamaica, Queens as an assistant teacher at an after-school program. The majority of the children who attended the program lived in houses with their families in the neighborhood while about a quarter of the students were living in the shelter where the program was held. Most of the younger children who lived in the shelter were incredibly happy and were a joy to be around. They knew they lived in a transitional space but they weren't aware of the societal stigmas that are attached to being homeless since they were so young, so they happily fit in with the other kids.

We have learned so many lies from the media and from brainwashed individuals in our life. This is inevitable. **It is our responsibility to wake up and question what influenced our perspectives on what is acceptable, what you desire and what makes you happy.** Only then, will we be able to truly understand and accept society as well as ourselves.

"Self-love comes in many forms but at its core it is an unconditional appreciation of one's self. Analyzing both flaws and strengths, and recognizing them for what they are without allowing outside perception is essential. Creating a protective, impenetrable shield that deflects harmful intentions allows us space for growth. Staring at ourselves, inside and out, to find beauty with our forever flaws gives us the room to improve what we need to and love what we can't. Be true to who you are. Be unapologetic about it. Love yourself unconditionally."

-Nay Marie, 33.

@tajimagazine

# TRUST YOU

Do you trust yourself? Trust must be earned, even when it comes to yourself. What makes YOU trust YOU? If you've been struggling and hurting your entire life and you haven't been able to help yourself, how can you trust yourself? If people have to show you that they are worthy and deserving of your trust, so do you.

Show yourself that you are deserving of your trust. Becoming discipline is a sure-fire way to earn your trust. Self-discipline, in the way I am using it, doesn't mean getting up for work at 6:30am every morning. That does involve a great amount of discipline, especially if you are not a morning person, but that is a different kind of discipline. It's easy to do what is expected of you. You HAVE to get up at 6:30 to make it to work by 8:00. You HAVE to go to class and complete your assignments to graduate. When society is in complete support of what you're doing, it is much easier and doesn't take much discipline to accomplish.

Self-discipline, in the way I'm using it, is when you train yourself to unlearn something that is imbedded in your psyche. When you pick up a new habit or practice that society may not necessarily support, it takes tremendous heart to pull through. That's why doing something that is expected of you, like getting up early for your day job, doesn't show great self-discipline. It is easy to go with the crowd and to live within their limitations of you. Self-discipline truly manifests when one decides to step out on faith and commit to something that goes against the grain, like a loc journey. When you relinquish yourself from societal norms regarding beauty standards and expectations, you are on a level of self-discipline which leads to high levels of self-love.

"Self-love is harder than loving any other being. It is fully embracing your soul and everything that comes with it- the good and the bad. Without the bad, we won't realize what's good. Without self-love, we can't truly love others. Be gentle and patient and you will find self-love."

-Julia Satin, 25.

@juliaelle_

# LOC JOURNEYS FOR SELF-LOVE

Committing to your loc journey shows self-discipline and helps build your trust in yourself which in turn develops your sense of self-love and confidence. When you walk against the herd of sheep, people may consider you crazy. They may call you weird and they may not understand you. That's okay. Your journey is not for their understanding. **Your journey is to help you discover your inner strength, true power and build great character.** The beginning stages help you develop remarkable resilience; grow a tougher skin to protect you from outward rejection and inward negativity.

I believe it's best to start your loc journey during a transitional period in your life. Stages of significance such as college, new parenthood, weight loss journey, marriage, divorce, loss of loved one, change in career path, relocating, retirement, recovery from illness or injury, etc. All of these transitions are significant and can be trying on you physically, mentally and emotionally. When dealing with such strenuous circumstances, it is always best to work on yourself. Often times we cleave to exterior stimuli for comfort, although we will never truly find the comfort we seek unless we find it within first.

Your loc journey builds your character and allows you to focus on yourself more instead of focusing all of your attention on those stressors mentioned above that can cause your self-worth to deteriorate. Starting your locs during a transition also helps you realize that your hair is not as important in your everyday life as you may have once thought.

Many people are reluctant to start their loc journey because they believe that they are too impatient to wait for their desired length. This is why starting your loc journey during a transitional period is ideal. You are killing two birds with one stone. When there is something more important taking your focus at times, the most difficult stages of the loc journey will pass you by without you having invested as much energy into letting the more awkward stages stress you out.

I often get comments from admirers saying things like "I love your locs. I couldn't wait for your length though but it's cool that you did." Wait for length? Nobody waits for their hair to grow. That's pathetic, a life to live where one awaits hair growth.

Yes, I keep track of my hair growth but I am not waiting. I am living.

I started my loc journey in college and I graduated on time with an internship under my belt at a health center doing HIV outreach, screening and counseling, involving myself in fashion shows and student panels. I had far too many things to consume my time and energy to sit around waiting for my hair to grow and loc. It's easier to put your energy into one pressing life transition while simultaneously starting your loc journey. You'll be better equipped to tackle your life transition since your hair transition demonstrates discipline and commitment, giving you confidence to accomplish all things.

"Being sexy is so much more than having your idea of the perfect body. Sexiness is more about an attitude. It is not braggadocios, in fact, cockiness is indicative of insecurities or overcompensation. Sexiness is knowing that you have flaws and knowing you are bad despite them."

-Keisha Charmaine Felix, 25 .

@killadoesthat

# LOCS & SEX APPEAL

For women, when we are starting off with our loc journeys and our locs are shorter, people looking on may not quite know what's going on with your hair. During your awkward and immature stage, especially when it's shorter, a lot of men will give you the side-eye, thinking 'what is going on with her head?' However, a lot of men will be very sure of the process you are going through and will acknowledge and honor you for it.

When I was starting off my locs, very often I would experience men off the street giving me words of encouragement like 'I see you, young queen' and 'I wish I would see more natural sisters like you, empress.' These comments I would often get from a certain type of man, men I like to call the *incense lighting, poetry reciting* type man. Of course, there's also the type of man that won't give you a second look. This is okay because as far as I'm concerned, that is not the man for you anyway. In general, a lot of men appreciate seeing a naturalista, whether she is rocking an afro or locs. Right off the bat men look at you and determine that you are a confident woman and that you are not overly concerned about others' opinions of you because if you were, you may have chosen to conform and wear a straight hairstyle or fake hair.

It is not the norm for women to wear their hair in its natural texture. It has become more popular in recent years however most black women still wear their hair straight. One thing that I love about wearing locs is that men will approach me with such respect and admiration. It feels nice, especially knowing that so many men conversely choose to approach women sexually immediately. Although calling women sexy is a compliment, we do not always want to be sexualized or viewed as sex objects so I appreciate when men choose to acknowledge and uplift a sister as beautiful, gorgeous, queen, empress, goddess, etc.

When you have locs and natural hair, as a woman, people have certain expectations of you. This goes for men and women who have these prejudgments. They want you to be "earthy". They want you to be wholesome. They want you to listen to neo-soul music by Jill Scott and Lauryn Hill. The minute you get caught twerking in the club, drinking Hennessey and rapping along with Nicki Minaj, they remove you from their mental pedestal and attack you. 'You're supposed to be my black queen but you're no longer worthy of my respect'. If you don't fit into the ideals of what a proud black sister with locs is supposed to be, it's an issue. 'Is that loc sister eating baby back ribs? Pork? Swine!?'

The respectability politics aspect of having locs, especially as a public figure, I find very difficult to maneuver. Besides being a woman with locs trying to inspire others to wear locs, I am a regular twenty-something year old black woman from around-the-way. I have made my share of mistakes and have my share of regrets. There are things I've done in my life that still bring up feelings of shame, bouts of depression and self-disgust. However, these experiences are common among young women who are learning themselves and learning the world around them. I don't try to empower black women because I feel like I am above them, I choose to empower them so that they remember they are not alone and maybe they can skip some of the struggles I've had and have a smoother transition into self-love and confidence. Being a naturalista, you do have to deal with people's expectations and judgments but that is something we face, as women especially, regardless of what style in which we choose to wear our hair.

In general, men are attracted to long hair. Growing locs is pretty much a sure-fire way to achieve a natural long hair style. Locs don't need to be trimmed frequently as loose hair does, nor do they have to deal with split ends as much that cause ends to break off easily. It can be tough to meet new people wearing baby locs, especially since **you** have ideas that **they** have ideas of who you are because of your hairstyle of choice. Your hair is short and a bit unruly and often doesn't give off the first impression you may desire. This is when the real you are able to shine through, when you are not leaning on a long-hair crutch.

Remember that above all, most men love confidence. Once you exude confidence, it doesn't matter what you have on your head. Be genuinely confident within your heart and soul and you will exude it. It is undeniable. Regardless of your hairstyle of choice, remember to be confident in your walk and your talk and you will have no problems attracting a mate. Self-love comes first, always.

"One of the most challenging lessons in life is knowing and understanding one's self, mentally, spiritually and emotionally. For some it may take months, years or even a lifetime."

-Destinee Lloyd, 25.

# BODY PARTY

I've been skinny practically my whole life. I was a chubby little baby and toddler but once I stopped drinking from a bottle, I slimmed down a lot. People have always made a big deal over my size, it was always quite annoying. They either hated it or loved it. Why most people had such polarizing views on my body, I never understood.

My elder family members would look at me and reminisce about the times when they were as slim as me in their youth. My family made me comfortable since it was normal for the young people to be skinny, I fit in. Strangers like my parents' co-workers and friends or even random people on the street made me feel uncomfortable with their comments.

"Do you eat?" That's a question I've always gotten and I still get it to this day. Of course I eat! Do you see the glow on my skin and the fullness of my hair!? I'm healthy! That's one of my biggest pet peeves. Most people don't understand how rude of a question that is. That is a question I typically get from black people, my people.

White people often refer to my size in admiration. 'I wish I could fit into your clothes' and 'wow, you must eat really healthy' are the types of comments I am accustomed to getting from white strangers and associates. When I catch people staring at my body for an extended period, in a seemingly non-sexual way, I imagine their thoughts. I picture black people thinking 'damn, she needs to eat' and I picture white people thinking 'damn, she has the perfect body.' Black people and white people have completely different standards of beauty when it comes to what's a desirable physique for a woman.

In different parts of the world, your weight says a lot about your socioeconomic status. In most underdeveloped countries, being skinny is a sign of poverty. Many poor people simply don't have enough food to eat so they are often underfed and underweight. Conversely, in a first world country like America, obesity is a trait associated with poverty. This is largely because in America, the cheapest foods are very fattening and easily accessible in low-income neighborhoods. Do these factors play a role into what we find attractive?

The black community always embraced thicker more voluptuous women more than slimmer women in my experience. This, coupled with the unsolicited comments about my size created some insecurities in me. I didn't get made fun of a lot in school since I was very well liked but every now and then I got teased. Everyone gets made fun of at some point at the schools I attended since Brooklyn kids love to 'cut ass' as we call it, or 'roast' each other. My size would be the only thing my peers would point out.

I was so torn. I was pursuing a modeling career. I was able to book fashion shows as a size 0 so my size was paying off in one respect, but I did not like feeling unattractive to my own people. For the past 10 years I've been practically the same weight. I recently worked up to a size 2 after prioritizing being at a healthier weight for my height and lifestyle. Of course, wanting to feel more attractive played a role in my weight gain but feeling comfortable in my own skin came first.

We all have different body image issues stemming from different sources. Some of us constantly receive unsolicited criticism, verbal harassment, sexual assault, etc., all reconfiguring the way we view our own bodies. So many people are getting plastic surgery to manipulate their bodies to the point where so many people look the same. Everyone has the right to manipulate their faces and bodies in whichever way they choose but I think it's important to consider why you have the feelings you do about the way you look. Once you fix your internal issues you may realize that your physical issues aren't really issues after all. We are all uniquely us, uniquely beautiful.

"Don't be afraid to feel pain. That's how you build endurance. That's how you grow your heart strong and open to love. People think closing your heart will protect you from heartache. I don't think so. A closed heart is always aching and will never be able to receive love. Don't fear the pain."

-Keisha Charmaine Felix, 25

@killadoesthat

"Let the mistakes of the past be a stepping stone to improve in the present and future."

-Jasmine Andrews, 26.

@jasminealyssaa

# FACING FEARS & INDECISION

Why are you scared? I don't mean scared of your loc journey but scared to make a change in your life where you are unhappy. So many people are constantly complaining about their lives while doing nothing to make a difference. They learn to become comfortable in their discomfort because it is familiar. This doesn't make any sense to me and it perpetuates a depressing prison-like climate in your life.

Making a change that you are hesitant about will be uncomfortable at first but the rewards could very well be worth your action if you allow it. I know if you are unhappy in your current circumstance, getting out of that will at least bring some relief.

It's a lot like deciding to break up with a significant other. You know the relationship isn't fulfilling but you've invested so much into it that you stay, comfortable in your discomfort. It's a familiar pain. You don't want to deal with the painful process of mourning the relationship and moving on, even though you'll have the relief of ending the relationship that was no longer serving you. You're fixated on the cons of leaving so you stay stuck in limbo, physically present but mentally elsewhere. Neglecting the fact that you will move on and your life will readjust from if you allow yourself the chance, you stick to the pain that you're used to out of fear.

Fear is the only thing worth being afraid of because it's the main road block in the way of people reaching their fullest potential. Insecurity is the seed that grows in the soil of fear.

I will not live my life vicariously through the people around me. One of the most sure-fire ways to become more confident is to face your fears. Are you afraid of heights? Get on that roller coaster. Are you afraid of drowning? Learn to swim. You won't overcome your fear and build your self-confidence by tippy toeing around the subject. You must face it head on. Challenge yourself. Every single day. Set goals then execute. Keeping your word to yourself shows integrity and gives you a reason to trust yourself, thus leading to a greater self-love.

A characteristic commonly associated with women is indecision. Constant indecision is a sign of low self-esteem and self-trust. I think it is important to practice decision making in all areas of life. When someone gives you a choice, don't say 'I don't know, what do you think?' Choose! Even in times when you are unsure, give yourself some time to decide but once that time has come and gone, make a decision, even if you are still unsure.

There will be times when you take too long to make a choice to the point where life ends up deciding for you. If you make the right decision, you will be proud that you trusted yourself. If you make the wrong decision, look for the lesson so that you can learn from your mistake. Either way, you asserted yourself and made a choice which shows great confidence. There are too many people living their lives in limbo, halfway out the door. **You can change nothing but nothing stays the same, so act in your own favor.** To build self-trust, you must… do. Go for it. Whether that be your loc journey or another journey. MOVE.

"As much as you think you need to, as much as you think you want to, you cannot do this 'greatness' thing by yourself. Lean back, trust God, and he'll equip you with what you need, Queen."

-Rukayatu Tijani, 27. @rukyoftheyear

# POWERFUL BEYOND MEASURE

So many things are lowering our vibrations and we don't even realize it. We feel anxious and don't even know what triggers our anxiety half of the time. I used to get high anxiety to the point where I'd waste my entire day in bed, feeling afraid and too insecure to step out of my house because… I don't even know! I would sit and watch TV and hear about all of these successful people and I'd feel happy for them and sorry for my miserable self at the same damn time!

It hit me like a James Brown beat. What's the big deal if I fail? The worst case scenario is that I'd be let off the hook for all of the responsibilities that come with succeeding. Succeeding is truly the scary part. Having found something worth aspiring towards, something worth fighting for, is a gift in itself. If you are lucky enough to have many blessings, which we all are, it is your duty to bless others. We could all be in unfortunate positions and would have to depend on the help of another.

We all love to listen to music, but what if those talented enough to play decided to keep their skills to themselves? It would be selfish not to share with the world all that you are capable of achieving. **You are bigger than you think you are. You are incredibly powerful. You are a creator and you matter!**

Once I started incorporating more fruits and vegetables into my diet, I started feeling more energized and alive. A smoothie is an easy way to get more live nutrition. Remember we are great but we are not machines to turn on and off as we please. What we put in is what we will get out. That also includes how we spend our pastime. Maybe one personality thrives off of watching horror movies but I know personally that wouldn't help me one bit. I live in New York City, isn't that scary enough?

Horror movies lower my vibration so I stay away from those. Along with sad songs, televised news and The Bad Girls Club. I am not shaming anyone who enjoys these things. Some spirits may thrive off those things but I have come to the awareness that mine does not. They make me feel drained and anxious. Evaluate what drains you and what energizes you. Once I cut those things out and made room for things that raised my vibration like jewelry making, guided meditations and comedies, my mood was better more often. You will discover your true power once you fuel yourself with the things that make you feel good. Feeling good is an easy way to feel confident in yourself.

"Don't be afraid to butterfly while others are cocooning. Your transformation and growth will inspire them one day to use their wings."

-Denequa Williams, 27.

@litbklyn

# THINK *NEGATIVE* THOUGHTS

I have had very vivid dreams for my entire life. In my younger years, I was very fascinated by the fact that I could escape reality and enter a whole new one. Not that I was in any circumstance that caused me to desire refuge, but I simply found it captivating. The endless possibilities. Back in my pre-pubescent years, I would have amazing adventures in my dreams. I would visit intriguing faraway lands and rub elbows with my favorite celebrities.

My dreams were so real. I can recall a morning I woke up and I was unsure about what my name was, momentarily, because I was being called Mary-Kate in a dream I had that previous night. I was about 9 years old and was a huge Olsen twins fan. When I had a dream that I remembered soon after awakening, I would write down everything about the dream that I could remember and relive the moment. In doing this practice, I had more meaningful dreams that I could recollect more often.

Over the years, I could spot a pattern in my dream journals. I noticed that I have more vivid dreams when I fall asleep right after being in deep thought about a person or situation. I have especially memorable and troubling dreams when I feel stressed out over an on-going problem in my life.

Recently I had a dream about my teeth falling out. Many believe that having dreams about losing teeth represent large amounts of stress and anxiety in your life. But it is always wise to analyze your dream for yourself to find symbolism and significance.

In this dream, I first noticed my wisdom teeth were feeling loose. Soon I noticed little by little, more and more teeth started feeling very loose, to the extent that I could not comfortably bite down as my teeth were no longer in alignment. I tried and tried to keep my teeth in place. As I went about my day, I forgot about what was happening to my teeth so I ended up doing something subtle that forced a tooth to fall completely out. Quickly I ended up with no teeth in my mouth at all, apart from some fragments in the front of my mouth.

I began to panic as I looked at my mouth in the mirror in horror. I thought to myself,

'Keisha, you look like a monster! Your career is over!' Then something clicked. I looked myself in the eye and suddenly I was back in the present moment. I said to myself, 'Keisha, it's okay. You are still beautiful. You may look a mess right now but this is temporary. You can go to the dentist tomorrow and find out what your options are then.' A feeling of relief swept over me and I woke up.

The morning I woke up from the dream was difficult. I couldn't stop thinking about my teeth falling out being a symbol of stress in my life. I kept thinking back to the things that were stressing me out and I would allow those thoughts to create debilitating anxiety. I came to a point where I realized, no, I cannot keep letting these thoughts ruin my days. I realized I had to defeat the thoughts.

**Think your negative thoughts through until you come to a positive outcome.** Most of us simply cannot stop thinking a negative thought, so I like to get to the root of the thought and find a positive gem in the soil. In this case, I got consumed in negative thoughts because my dream about my teeth falling out reminded me of all my stressors. My dream also showed that I can work through stressful thoughts by stepping outside of this current moment of fear so that I could step inside a state of calm.

Unfortunately, I ignored the positive ending and was stuck on the negative. Though my teeth fell out, it only harmed me to focus on not having teeth anymore and the negative consequences that could potentially come with that. Once I started thinking of visiting the dentist and the ways he could possibly fix my teeth, I felt relief. It helped me to think of what I could do to solve the problem and bring hope and faith into the situation rather than dwell on the issue itself.

Don't just dismiss a negative thought because it will constantly come back. It could also grow and cause a negative impact on other areas of your life. Tackle it head on. Is the negative thought an insecurity? Think about that insecurity and the root cause of why you have it. Are your insecurities based on external views that were inflicted upon you? Realize why those views were inflicted on you and the thousands of people who have the exact same insecurity. Deconstructing your socialization is a great way to unlearn your insecurities. To deconstruct, you must break down your feelings and think through those negative thoughts to come to an understanding, a re-learning and a positive state of mind.

"Don't ask anyone to show you your worth. You should be the first example of what it looks like to love, honor and adore you."

-Renee Edwards, 25. @nusbeauty

# THE CONSEQUENCES OF SELF-LOVE

One sad truth that comes with human nature is that most people would rather sit back and watch rather than get up and do for themselves. They like to live vicariously through others' success because of their fears of their own success. Unfortunately, this doesn't only come with admiration but it involves much envy and hatred.

It makes people uncomfortable to see another person genuinely happy, living in their truth, expressing themselves fully and loving themselves wholeheartedly. Instead of reflecting on their own short comings, they would rather project their own insecurities and call out what they see to be flawed of the fearless self-lover. Some of the worst hate is manifested in people who believe that their own ideals must be universal. These people will attack your character and your morals without an ounce of consideration for how their disrespect reflects on their own character.

Once you start to love yourself more and more, those around you may notice a difference in your energy. It may make them uncomfortable because being familiar with your lack of self-love made them comfortable with theirs. Misery loves company after all. Expect that some people will try to shame you for your change in behavior but don't let that deter you on your self-love journey. One will never reach the mountain top without encountering obstacles along the path.

Consider the negativity you face from the people in your life as tests. Their negativity will challenge your progress so it is important to always remember that your self-love journey is for you to become your own greatest version.

You may have to cut toxic people out of your life. Are you having difficulty identifying who in your life is toxic? If you feel like someone is depleting you and not replenishing you, they are toxic. If you believe your relationship is based on what they can get from you, they are toxic. If someone is consistently negating your aspirations, they are toxic. If you are always there to provide a helping hand or a shoulder to lean on and they don't provide that for you in return, they are toxic.

There is no reciprocity with toxic people. People often display different representations of themselves to different people so I don't want to necessarily label an individual as toxic. However, if there is no reciprocity in different aspects of your relationship where you need it and they leave you feeling drained, they are toxic for you.

"Where did my magic go?

She felt as though she'd lost her "touch". The ability to make anything appear at her whim and be happy.

That is what most people mistake about magic, my love. It does not just "appear".

It is the seemingly impossible birthed into existence through negotiations between entities.

It is magic to most because its appearance is awesome & unbelievable, given the circumstances it arrived in.

Mais, it is the labor of negotiations, compromise, struggle & resoluteness that is the magic. It's veneer a reflection of that work.

Entonces, you must prepare yourself to conceive and grow the magic you miss while remaining true to me, your fire, through it all.

You carry all of the ingredients & are capable of rebuilding it to shine again."

(excerpt from Love Conversations Between Ori + Me)

-Sawdayah Brownlee, 27.

@africanherbsmaam

# SWEET SOLITUDE

I've struggled with making irrational decisions because my 'intuition' told me to do something. It's foolish to always go with your instincts because often that gets us into trouble. But our intuition and our instincts are supposed to be our natural inherent senses to help us not hinder us, right? Absolutely. But when our intuition is clouded with insecurities, it is not trustworthy. When we overthink and overanalyze, we overlook the truth which is often very simple. I can make a crack in the sidewalk seem like the Grand Canyon after a conversation with the angel and the demon over my shoulders. It gets real bad when there's a demon on both shoulders, one encouraging me to do damage and the other saying cause destruction.

With enough trial and error, I have come to the realization that I cannot simply trust my intuition until I cultivate it. Rather than being reactionary, it's best to take a moment to reflect, get an awareness of one's feelings and see if those feelings are truly justified. It is important to see how our feelings influence our decision making. I am working to be better at communicating my feelings instead of speaking or acting impulsively, using intellect over emotion. Respond, don't react.

Throughout the day, I check in with myself by asking 'Keisha, how are you feeling?' I tend to be moody so it's helpful to be mindful of my emotional states and what is the cause or trigger of each mood. It helps me decide if I should feel one way or another. It also helps me to think myself out of negative thoughts so I can actively and genuinely get myself in a better mood.

Have you ever tried to not think? I know, sounds impossible if you aren't familiar with meditation but it is incredibly important to quiet your mind in this world where we have so many external factors interfering with our inner peace. We have thousands of thoughts in a day, so many of them are unproductive and stifling. Most of us struggle with anxiety at some time or another. Quieting the mind helps to silence negative thoughts, encouraging a more blissful state of being.

Quieting the mind is a skill one can develop over time with dedicated practice. The easiest way to learn to meditate is through guided meditations. A leader will direct your breathing or create imagery for you to visualize. There is a ton of guided meditations available online for you to listen to as well as apps that you can download to your phones which are great for calming your mind and body from stressful states.

It is so important to be comfortable in your own company. It is in this time of stillness where you will be able to have a clear mind to be able to hear God's messages and learn yourself. Creating a ritual is essential. Whether it's something you do a few times a day to a few times a month, develop some sort of a routine that involves only you. Journaling, exercising, spa trips, going to the theater, and listening to music are all things that I do during my me-time. Spending time alone will help you learn yourself and learn what it is you need in life.

Neediness and clinginess is a sign of insecurity and immaturity. Naturally, human beings need love from another but without being independent outside of that relationship, we'll have too much of ourselves invested in someone else. This is dangerous. Other people having so much power in your life can be detrimental. When your self-love is strong, romantic love from another is not a need but an added bonus.

"Shifting. Cracking. Breaking. Bursting feminine emotional GOLD at the creative seams. Flowing. Pouring. Abundantly refreshing… to feel. To embrace yourself, even through the pain. What a gift child… to hit the rockiest bottom of your soul and wake up in the palm of your highest self."

-sapoDILLA, 24.

@sapodillaunleashed

# FEMININE ENERGY

Black women are very often the head of the household. Being raised by single mothers, black girls grow up with a certain masculinity that is often overlooked and underexamined. Especially black girls raised by single black mothers in urban communities. We often take on the role of a man in different aspects of our lives as black men are often absent or inconsistently present. This can cause young women to neglect the divine feminine within.

The subject of gender roles today is taboo but we cannot ignore the fact that in families, the mother and father typically have different responsibilities. Whether directly or indirectly, a father will show his children how a man treats a woman in ways that a mother simply cannot teach. If a daughter is raised without a male head (or other father figures in her family, in the form of older brothers, cousins, uncles or grandfathers) she will likely grow up believing that men are unnecessary in families.

I witnessed my parents struggling together as husband and wife, living in a basement apartment and I also witnessed my mother thriving as a single mother and homeowner after their divorce. In many ways, this showed me that if a man isn't helping me reach my potential, he is useless. I believed that I won't need a man in my life if I can take care of myself. If my mother was able to take care of herself and my siblings, I can do the same. Men will just drain my resources and energy without replenishing me with a thing. We black women are often higher educated and higher paid than black men so we can take care of business on our own.

This was my train of thought for a very long time and this mentality played a major role in the demise of many friendships and relationships I've had with black men. Whenever I saw the slightest sign of incompatibility or a character flaw, I would be quick to run away because I believed if the relationship or friendship isn't perfect, it's not worth the headache since I didn't believe I needed a man in my life, outside of my brother and uncles, anyway.

This way of thinking is terribly flawed. No, I may not need men to provide for me financially but I need men to provide balance. I embrace my femininity fully and nothing can make me feel quite like a woman than a masculine man. But it is important to be prepared to receive masculine energy for it to be beneficial in the ways that we may want. **The men we attract are reflections of ourselves, so it's very important to blossom into yourself before seeking a man to complete you.** Nobody can complete you. Relationships flourish when two complete people come together or when two people grow to completion together. It's funny how much you can learn about yourself from your relationships, romantic or otherwise.

Black women often reject love when we receive it. It is not because we don't want love but sometimes we have great difficulty identifying real love. This is often because of the pain we may have endured from people who were supposed to have loved us. So we stay in messy and dangerous situations because it is familiar; messy and dangerous "love" is the only love we see firsthand, in many cases. We'll learn to accept real love once we learn how it feels to receive real love from ourselves. Our standards will rise and the people on your frequency will follow suit.

"I'm not a part of all this chaos. I Am a Divine being that is one with the universe."

-Danielle Loxs, 26. @ladiswagg55

# I AM WELL

I was in 9th grade. It was early September and I still had my 'first-day-of-school' anxiety which I was trying to work through. Sitting in English class, I began to get serious cramping in my abdominal region, cramping that I could not understand or explain. I felt crippled. The class period ended and almost everyone left the classroom except for me and my new friend Sasha. She saw tears in my eyes and knew I was in some sort of pain. My school didn't have a nurse so she helped me to the main office as I could barely stand upright on my own.

> "What's wrong with you, do you have your period? Are you pregnant?" Asked one of the aids.

> "I don't have my period and no, I'm not pregnant." I replied with an attitude, annoyed that my school didn't have a nurse. I wasn't due for my period at the time and a pregnancy, beyond Immaculate Conception, was impossible.

> "Well, I can't give you a pain reliever so do you want me to call an ambulance or call

your mom to come pick you up?" She asked rather impatiently.

"Call my mom, I guess." I decided reluctantly since I knew my mother would be inconvenienced by coming downtown Brooklyn to pick me up but I didn't want to go to the hospital. My mom was in the middle of teaching and said she'd come when school was out. It was towards the end of the day so I wouldn't have to wait very long.

I sat in the noisy office, keeled over, looking pretty pathetic and feeling sorry for myself. Then a woman walked in the office with the intention of picking up her niece. She realized it was in the middle of the class period so she decided to wait until it was over, since it was the final period of the day. She was full of smiles and I could tell she was probably a talker so I was annoyed when she sat next to me, knowing she would start a conversation. I was right.

"Why aren't you in class young lady?" She asked very politely.

"I'm sick." I consciously kept my response brief and avoided eye contact so she could tell that I wasn't interested in chit chat.

"No." She replied.

I was confused. What did she mean 'no'? I said I was sick, what sort of response is that? I hadn't wanted to converse but I was intrigued. "Excuse me?" I asked with concern.

"Don't say you're sick. There is power in 'I am', say 'I am well', say it." She spoke with so much self-assurance that I obliged, though apprehensive. I wondered if anyone else in the office could hear our exchange.

>"I'm well?"
>
>"Don't ask it, declare it."
>
>"I'm well."
>
>"Say it again."
>
>"I'm well."

"That's much better. So, this is an art school. What do you do?" She changed the subject and I was relieved because I wasn't comfortable with how the conversation was going.

"I'm a dancer, ballet. But this school doesn't offer ballet. I like to draw though," I said.

"Yes! I've been looking for an artist to draw my husband! I want a big drawing of him as Moses parting the Red Sea," she told me and I was sure she was nutty. But she drew me in with her mesmerizing Erykah Badu eyes.

"Well, I don't know if I can draw that." I said wearing my self-doubt on my sleeve.

"Of course you can, I'll pay you," she said. I thought such a commission was too advanced for my talent but I decided I would try anyway.

"Okay, I'll do it." I perked up and decided to take on the challenge. She was pleased and gave me a piece of paper to write down my contact information. She wanted my cell number, my email address and my AIM screenname. This was back in 2005 when people were using instant messages over text messages.

Class let out, her niece came and they left together. My mother showed up shortly after.

"You look real sick," my mother said sarcastically. At this point, the pain I felt had subsided tremendously. I got home, drank some soup, took a nap and felt much better. When I woke up, I was constantly checking my phone and email with hopes of hearing from the lady. I realized she never told me her name, nor did she give me any of her contact information. Several days went by and I didn't hear from her. In fact, I never heard from her.

For a while, I was disappointed that she didn't reach out to me like she said she would. For a few years I thought back to meeting that woman, upset that she changed her mind, until it hit me. She never had any intentions on commissioning me to draw her husband parting the Red Sea as Moses did in the book of Exodus. Her only intention was to lift my spirits since I was sitting in that office looking miserable. She wanted me to feel better mentally so that I would feel better physically. And it worked.

She was the first person that I can recall to teach me the power of affirmations. God told Moses, "I am that I am" in Exodus and we, too, are what we say we are. If we say something enough, with the intention of believing it, it becomes truth. Our words, especially the words we use about ourselves, do manifest, positive or negative.

The emotion and intention behind our words play a significant role in our manifestations. **Languages vary all over the world but emotions are universal.** God knows your heart and your intentions. God sees your commitment and efforts. Speak self-love into existence. Speak all your truest desires into existence. Visualize it. What would you look like if you were living in a greater sense of self-love? How would you walk? How would you talk? How would your posture be? Where would you spend your time, and with whom? Close your eyes and see it with emotions of gratitude as if you are already there. Always stay gracious, for God will not give you more, if you cannot appreciate what he's already given you.

The phrase, 'perception is reality', is true. One can choose to see the glass half empty or see the glass half full, but the fact remains that there are two halves to the glass. The glass is both half empty and the glass is also half full. Whichever half you choose to focus on is up to you but remember, your perspective will shape your experiences. Choose happy. Choose you. Have a blessed journey =.)

Here are some of my favorite affirmations.
WARNING: Side effects may include an increased sense of gratitude, joy, prosperity and abundance.
Recite daily at your own risk.

I am well

I am magnificent

I am deserving

I am brave

I am strength

I am faith

I am wise

I am inspiration

I am successful

I am love

I am light

I am beauty

I am wealth

I am health

I am intuitive

I am trust

I am worthy

I am enough

I am important

I am peace

I am creation

I am innovation

I am brilliance

I am real

I am freedom

I am spirit

I am glorious

I am motivation

I am determination

I am nature

I am elevation

I am eternal

I am compassion

I am grace

I am joy

I am peace

I am trust

I am hope

I am courage

I am forgiveness

I am gratitude

I am possibility

I am poise

I am eternal

I am elevation

I am amazing

I am proud

I am found

I am secure

# PHOTO GALLERY

(photographed by Chioma Nwana)

Play with curls! Curls will add beautiful volume and romance to your lovely locs.

I love to caress my hair.

It's beautiful, it's mine!

Get into my maze of a mane!

Curls and new-growth is a recipe for thickness!

Looking into the future and it's mighty bright over there.

I am more and more grateful as the days go on, and my hair grows long.

No two locs are the same. My locs are uniquely mine.

My hair is kinky, it grows towards the sun!

I am happy, unapologetically so.

I'm wearing my original Love, Light & Locs jewelry.

Every day I live my dreams.

I am a magnet for prosperity, love and joy.

My locs and my original jewelry, up-close and personal.

Though I love to experiment with loc styles, wearing my hair down makes me feel free.

My locs flourish no matter the season.

Waist length locs of almost 7 years.

My locs have different textures.

My hair is curly, coily and kinky.

I love the woman I am growing into.

Natural hair care is self-care.

Healthy hair is good hair, regardless of its texture.

The twists in my locs are two thinner locs that I combined into one thicker loc.

My locs represent my self-love journey.

# LOVE, LIGHT & LOCS

(Part II: Loc Maintenance Tips)

There is a wealth of knowledge available for properly caring for natural black hair but the information available for cultivating and maintaining locs is very scarce and often very general. After reading Part II, you'll be able to walk away with a greater understanding of how locs are formed, discover if locs are for you, learn how to deal with common issues that may arise on your loc journey, how to wash, style, maintain your locs at different stages in your loc journey and so much more.

# WHY AM I SO PASSIONATE ABOUT LOCS?

Everyone locks their hair for different reasons. Locs represent a lifestyle or religion for some people. To others, locs represent one's spiritual identity. Locs help people embrace their ethnicity and help them accept who they believe they were meant to be. To many people, locs are an edgy fashion statement. Maybe locs are a form of rebellion to some. A lot of people choose locs for convenience alone.

Regardless of the reason people choose to lock their hair, we locked naturals are a community. We have needs and desires concerning maintenance, products and representation. I love being able to help bring us together to build a forum for us to share our ideas for one another. Regarding representation, many of us don't believe we need the acceptance of others but without people understanding locs on a mainstream level, we face discrimination and prejudice for our decision to wear an "alternative" hairstyle from people both black and white.

I choose to be an advocate for locs since it's a style that I find incredibly beautiful and unique which is worn by everyone including doctors, actors, engineers, athletes, lawyers, musicians, etc. and yet there are still so many negative stigmas attached to locs and people who wear them. I hope to help crush the stigmas associated with locs by informing individuals about locs, loc maintenance and encourage more love for the locked community.

# SHOULD YOU LOCK YOUR HAIR?

Attention class, put your books away and take out your No. 2 pencils. It's time for a pop quiz! Don't worry, you can breathe easy since your grade on this quiz won't be reflected on your report card. Based on your answers, I will help you determine if locs are a great hairstyle choice for you. Choose True or False for the following 10 questions.

1) I like to change my hairstyles frequently. One week I like to wear curls and the next week I like to wear my hair straight.
   TRUE or FALSE
2) I don't do much with my look. I like to keep it simple on most days and maybe I'll switch it up with something fancy for a special occasion.
   TRUE or FALSE
3) I live a very active lifestyle. I am very busy and don't have much time to dedicate to doing my hair.

TRUE or FALSE
4) I exercise frequently. I need a hairstyle that will allow for me to wash it often and not ruin my hairstyle since I sweat so much.
TRUE or FALSE
5) I am indecisive about my desired hair length. Sometimes I like to wear it short and sometimes I like to wear it long.
TRUE or FALSE
6) I love my natural hair and I enjoy putting a lot of tender love and care into my hair maintenance.
TRUE or FALSE
7) Hair is just hair to me. It is not important to my life and I don't care what it looks like.
TRUE or FALSE
8) I'm not really much of an advocate for natural hair. I like wigs, weaves and extensions.
TRUE or FALSE
9) My natural self is my truest self. I love looking the way God intended me to look without manipulation.
TRUE or FALSE
10) I like hair color. Black hair is beautiful but I want to dip and dabble in other colors like blonde and red too.
TRUE or FALSE

## The results are in!

If you chose mostly TRUE, locs are perfect for you!
If you chose mostly FALSE, locs are perfect for you!
If you chose half TRUE and half FALSE, locs are perfect for you!

Okay, maybe I tricked you a little bit but I promise I had good intentions. This quiz was made to simply show that locs are incredible for so many different types of people. I will touch upon the surface below, but please note that they will be discussed further throughout the book. Always remember to address your health concerns with your primary care physician.

**Versatility.**

Locs are incredibly versatile. If you like to switch up your hairstyles often, you can absolutely do that with locs. You can wear your locs short, long, cut into a bob or create a faux bob. You can also create a faux pixie cut! You can curl your locs, crimp them, create waves or wear them straight. You can make all types of braids, twists, cornrows, flat twists, bantu knots, loc knots, buns, ponytails, up-dos, side-dos, pompadours, basket weaves, barrel rolls, pin curls and so much more especially if you go to a skilled loctician. You are liable to leave the salon with a style you've never seen before.


**Simplicity.**

Although you can do so much with your locs, you don't have to if that isn't your personal style. Locs are also incredibly beautiful if you wear your hair down, in a bun or a ponytail every single day. You can wear your hair in simple hairstyles with your locs, be comfortable and look great!


**Quickness.**

For those of you with very busy lives, locs are very convenient. You can style your locs once between your washes and keep that style throughout your busy schedule. As long as you maintain your locs well while you sleep, your style will be as fresh as new until it's time for wash day.

**Exercise.**

Many people work-out regularly or swim regularly so their scalps and roots are often wet from sweat and water. There are also many of us who simply enjoy letting water run through our hair every now and then when we shower. Locs are a great solution to maintaining your hair if you often deal with a wet head. Those who interlock their locs will consistently have groomed locs since water won't cause your roots to unravel which can be a major concern. If you allow your locs to dry completely, your hair will be in good shape.

**Length changes.**

If you desire to wear short hairstyles or long hairstyles and you like to go back and forth between the two, locs are a great way to do so. There are many ways to style your long locs to give the appearance and illusion of a shorter haircut. You can also wear braid and twist extensions over your locs to get the look of long hair.

**Wigs & extensions.**

Just because you wear your hair in a natural style, it doesn't mean that you have to be #teamnatural every single day. If you want to wear wigs over your locs you can do so. With short locs you can easily fit your locs under a wig when you please. Although it is more difficult, there are different techniques to fit long locs under wigs with the assistance of a wig cap and even a needle and thread. Braid, twist, and faux loc extensions are also very easy to add onto your locs on your own or with the help of a friend or hairstylist.

**Maintenance.**

The amount of energy you place into maintaining your locs is completely up to you. You can go the minimalist route and use no products, simply water, and potentially thrive. Others may want or need to take the time out to experiment with different products and techniques to wash, groom and moisturize their hair. It is completely up to you. As long as you take the time to learn what your hair needs and likes, you can make the appropriate accommodations for it. The time you take into caring for your hair can be extremely therapeutic and is a great addition to your self-care routine.

**Freeforming.**

Freefrom locs are locs that are cultivated most naturally. They form on their own without much manipulation. At most, they are washed, moisturized and sometimes pulled or separated into different directions. They are rarely, if ever, twisted. Some people choose to live their lives organically in many different ways. Freeforming is a great method to achieve organic locs.

**Spirituality.**

Many people tie locs to their spirituality as they can represent one's personal growth and their connection to their higher power as antennae. There are tons of different spiritual and religious correlations with locs and whichever, if any, may resonate with you is beautiful.

**Hair color.**

Just like other types of hair, you can use over the counter dyes, semi-permanent and permanent colors, to change your hair color as you desire. Beware of the potential long term side effects of using bleach on your locs. Go to a professional if you are not confident in your abilities to color your hair yourself.

# WHAT ARE LOCS? & HOW ARE THEY FORMED?

Locs are the result of allowing your hair to mat together without detangling. This can happen through intentional manipulation or neglect. Over time hair will mat together, whether naturally or by force, producing what we often refer to as dreadlocks, dreads or locs. The pace of which one's hair locks is determined by many factors including hair texture, method of locking, maintenance during the locking process (such as retwisting or washing), hair length and the health of your hair prior to locking.

Some of the most common ways that people form their locs are by parting their hair and creating comb coils. This method is most common among people with coarsely textured hair (4a-4c) at shorter lengths. Comb coils are perfect for kinky hair textures as naturally tight curl patterns hold comb coils very well and it trains your hair to stay in a cylindrical shape.

Two more common methods of starting locs are two-strand twists or braid-locs. These are most common among people with longer hair as long coils tend to unravel more often on longer hair. Interlocking is a common way to start locs on more loosely curled hair (3a-3c hair types). Using a tool such as a latch hook to create knots throughout the length of the strands is a great way to begin locs on loose textured hair as this hair type tends to unravel rather quickly.

For locking straight hair, backcombing is highly recommended. This is when you comb your hair towards the roots to encourage tangling since straight hair doesn't hold a twist, braid or coil very well. This will create frizz which should be wrapped around the loc to encourage the desired cylindrical shape.

Using a loc sponge, or a large sponge with small holes cut out of it, a great tool to start locs on very short kinky hair. It is most common among men and most convenient with hair that is about an inch long or even shorter.

It has become very popular to start locs with faux loc extensions, and as the natural hair grows out, it is twisted and groomed.

Last but not least, it is common to start locs by leaving your hair alone. No manipulation will result in organic freeform locs.

# STARTING LOCS WITH HEALTHY HAIR

Regardless of the method that you choose to begin your locs, it is best to start with healthy hair. You may need to have at least an inch of natural hair before starting your locs depending on your method of choice. Consider the method that you want to choose to begin your journey when considering how long your hair should be, or consider how long your natural hair already is when considering what method to start your locs.

Your locs will thrive if your natural hair thrives. Oh yeah, that reminds me, start with natural hair! If your hair is chemically straightened, it is highly recommended that you either transition to natural or shave your hair and grow out your natural texture prior to locking. I have heard success stories from people who started their locs with permed hair but the permed hair may not give you your desired look or texture and it will give you issues in the future with dryness and excess breakage which can occur at the worst times, causing embarrassment. You can easily skip that struggle by waiting until your natural hair grows to a length that you're comfortable with to start your locs. No pressure, the decision is yours.

Same goes for dyed hair. I would recommend that you start your locs on hair that is not chemically processed in any way, including hair dye. Many people have successfully started their locs with color treated hair. However I must point out that dyed hair requires frequent conditioning or else it can become extremely dry and brittle. Conditioning starter locs can encourage unravelling as most conditioners have a lot of slip and are designed to detangle so it can slow down the locking process. However, I will still suggest that you use conditioner on your starter locs sporadically but I will discuss that in depth further into the book. So again, the decision is yours.

# MYTHS DEBUNKED

If you are a loc beginner, you may have learned a lot of misinformation about locs and how they should be maintained. Before you start improperly cultivating and grooming your locs, check out these untruths to get a better understanding of the proper way to care for your locs.

1) You're Not Supposed to Wash Your Locs

    If this were true, boy would that be disgusting! Do you have any idea of the amount of things hair comes into contact with that needs to be washed out on a regular basis? Air pollution, dust, products, sweat, dead skin and so much more. One cannot maintain a healthy scalp to produce healthy hair growth without washing as needed. I recommend that you shampoo your locs and scalp nearly as often as you would shampoo your loose natural hair. People don't consider the fact that regardless of the way you choose to wear your hair, your scalp is still the same and you may very need to maintain it the same.

Where did this myth come from and why do people believe you're not supposed to wash locs? Many stylists will recommend that their clients refrain from washing their locs for the first several months of their loc journey so that their hair doesn't unravel. Contrary to popular belief, this will actually slow down the locking process. The act of washing and retwisting helps the hair lock together faster. The water may cause immediate unraveling but it helps the hairs to mat together. This process followed by retwisting gives your locs a trained and uniform appearance which is often desired. There are ways to wash your locs to minimize unraveling. (See page 183)

2) You Are Not Supposed to Use Conditioner

Many locticians will make this very suggestion because conditioner is a big culprit, causing product build-up in your locs. In my opinion, rather than teaching people not to use products, I believe it is better to teach them how to properly clean their locs so that products don't cause build-up. I recommend using conditioner on mature locs especially if they are color treated. I wouldn't suggest that conditioner be used every single wash to help avoid product buildup but every other wash is how I prefer to maintain my color treated locs of about 7 years. For people who prefer cleaner, more pure products, hot oil treatments are the perfect alternative to condition your locs. (See page 193)

3) You Must Use Beeswax to Loc Your Hair

This couldn't be further from the truth. Beeswax is a product commonly used to form locs and tame frizz. Although many people choose to use beeswax, by no means is beeswax the only medium to cultivating locs. It is actually highly suggested to refrain from using beeswax for a number of reasons. Beeswax is very sticky and it remains sticky long after your hair has been groomed. This will cause dirt and dust to bond to your locs, causing dirt build-up over time. Wax is difficult to wash out of locs and often it is not washed out completely, causing stubborn product build-up.

In reality, hair, regardless of texture, will loc on its own without the aid of any product's assistance. That's just what hair does when you leave it alone or when you train it to lock by avoiding detangling. So of course you don't need to use beeswax on your hair. Most of us opt to use gels instead if we use products at all. There is an abundance of gels on the market to try out to discover which products are best for your needs. Remember, locs will lock regardless of any miraculous product you are sold. Many people only use water to lock their hair and that is perfectly fine as long as washing with shampoo is still a part of regular maintenance.

4) Locs Destroy Your Edges

Upon observing many people with locs, you may notice thinning around their edges and a receding hairline. This is usually caused by excessive retwisting. It is recommended that you retwist once every 2 weeks at most to preserve a healthy hairline. It is likely that retwisting any more often than that can cause traction alopecia, which is baldness often caused by over styling and tight styling. There are ways to nurse a balding hairline back to life and fullness however the bald spots that you may suffer are often irreversible. In which case, some people opt to get hair transplants to replenish their hairline as a more permanent solution or use fibers or makeup to temporarily fill in their edges.

If you prefer to always have a "fresh" looking appearance around your edges, I recommend that you pay special care during your bedtime routine to help care for your edges overnight to ensure freshness in the morning (See page 195). Locs are not a death sentence for your edges and your hairline, have no fear.

5) Locs Are Heavy!

Well first let's address the fact that words like heavy and light are relative terms so each individual has their own judgment regarding what is heavy to them. With that being said, we must take into consideration the fact that we all have different hair textures, thicknesses and hair densities which will all play a role in the weight of our locs. Unless you get extensions one day, your locs will gradually get longer and heavier so you may hardly notice a change in its weight. Your body will be prepared to handle the weight since it comes on so slowly. If you find that the weight of your locs is noticeably straining you, you may want to consider trimming them and maintaining a certain length for your comfort.

Also, the cleanliness of our locs will play a major role when it comes to how heavy our locs feel. You know the feeling you get when you eat a ton of food and then you finally relive yourself in the bathroom? You feel much lighter and freer, right? It's the same with locs. If you use a lot of products on your locs and don't wash very often, your locs will feel heavier. Locs will also feel heavier while soaking wet. Remember, locs are much like sponges. Once they are freshly cleaned and dried, then your locs will feel much lighter than they did while they were dirty and wet.

6) Locs Are Permanent

I like to refer to locs as a semi-permanent hairstyle. It is permanent to the extent that once your locs are done forming into mature locs, the length of your locs will not simply unravel. No matter how often they are submerged in water or how much detangling conditioner you use, your locs will stay locked. However, with effort and intent, you can comb-out your locs.

Obviously, this is something that you may want to think long and hard about before committing to combing them out since you dedicated so much time and energy into locking your hair in the first place. Locs take months to form but can be combed out in the matter of hours. So although locs are permanent in terms of you needing not to re-lock all of your hair when you wash and maintain them, they are not permanent since

you can comb them out whenever you desire
to embrace your loose tresses.

# SHRINKAGE

A major factor involved in understanding your loc journey is understanding shrinkage. If you've had loose natural hair for some time before starting your locs, then you may very well understand the concept. Shrinkage has a lot to do with the spring effect of your curl pattern. The curlier or kinkier your hair, the more shrinkage you may experience. Your tresses must intermingle to lock and that can't be done without shrinkage.

You may start your locs with your hair at a certain length expecting your locs to be that long, however as your hair mats together, it shrinks up. So when locking your hair, expect that it may appear shorter and shorter before it starts to show the length that you grow.

You may be tempted to pull on your locs as you notice them starting to appear shorter however it is best if you refrain. The early shrinking process is a vital part of your loc journey. Without this step, your locs simply will not lock. If you constantly pull on your shrinking locs to see how long they appear while stretched, you'll interrupt the shrinking process and slow it down. That is one of the reasons why some of the best loc advice you'll ever hear is to leave your hair alone while they are locking.

Once you get your locs installed, of course continue to maintain your hair and scalp hygiene, groom regularly and as desired however outside of these few instances, leave your hair alone. The early stages of locking your hair is for training your hair to mat into locs, so try not to make styling a priority as the pulling can disturb the process.

The shrinkage process will start with budding. A bud in your locs is the nucleus so to speak. Once you notice a knot in your locs, your locs are truly starting to form. You may not always notice the bud with your eyes but you should be able to feel it with your fingers. Sometimes the bud will look like a bean or a seed in your locs, in which case you'll be able to see it as it may protrude much like a pregnant woman's belly. In the instances where you can't see the bud, it'll feel like a mass inside of the loc. Many people's locs bud midway through the length but this will vary greatly.

At this point, you've learned that your locs will shrink as they mat together. They will appear shorter although they are growing as your hair normally grows. Your locs will also get thicker as they shrink and retain shed hair. They will swell as they begin to mature as teenage locs and then once they are fully locked, they will likely find a medium as they become more compact.

While you may become impatient dealing with a stagnant length during the early shrinkage stages, remember that once you've gotten the majority of the shrinkage out of the way, your locs will have a bit of weight to them and they'll start to appear longer. Many people claim to experience a growth spurt once their locs become fully locked but others may argue that your hair isn't actually growing any more than average, but since your hair isn't shrinking into itself as much and the weight of your locs is gently pulling your hair downwards, it appears as though you experience a growth spurt. I prefer to refer to that stage as a length spurt rather than a growth spurt since I don't believe your hair actually grows faster than usual.

# WASHING LOCS

Washing your locs is a vital activity to encourage healthy hair locking. When starting your locs, remember that washing your locs regularly is necessary and should not be skipped because of your fear of unraveling. I highly recommend putting your hair in a stocking cap and washing your hair through the material. This will help to keep your locs intact while you cleanse them. If you choose to use conditioner on your starter locs, I suggest you only do so through a stocking cap.

Conditioner, although it's purpose is primarily to provide lasting moisture and softness, often has detangling ingredients which will cause unraveling. Once your locs start budding significantly, then you should feel confident in washing them freely without the aid of a stocking cap. You'll be able to differentiate between your locs when it's time to retwist.

When washing your locs, remember to fully saturate them with water before adding any soaps, shampoos or conditioners. This will help ensure that the products are distributed well throughout your hair and will rinse out fully as well. Massage your scalp with your fingertips to gently lift any sweat, flakes or dirt without damaging your roots and follicles. It is common practice to scratch your scalp with your nails to clean it however that will likely cause breakage at the root and cause minor cuts on your scalp which will interrupt healthy hair growth. Massage your hair and scalp as if you were handwashing a delicate and expensive piece of fabric. Your hair is precious so don't scrub it so vigorously as you would scrub a frying pan.

When washing your locs, it is often difficult to know if you have fully rinsed out all of the shampoo and conditioner. Locs are very good at holding onto product so when you think you've washed out your locs fully, rinse again. Often times, locs tend to hold onto shampoo and conditioner towards the roots where the loose new growth meet your locked hair, about an inch from your scalp. When rinsing out the product, make sure to pay special attention to this part of your locs to make sure you don't leave the wash without tackling any product that may be left behind. Leaving product in your locs will later attract dirt and dust, leaving your hair with a dirty look (See page 197).

We love washing our hair with warm to hot water because we believe that in conjunction with our shampoo, we're eliminating the grease and dirt in the best way. However, hot water leads to excess frizziness in hair and especially locs in particular. This can be prevented by using cool water during your final rinse to seal the shafts of your strands to help prevent frizz (See page 204).

# MILDEW & DRYING LOCS

Who would have thought your method of drying your locs would play a major role in the health of your locs and its physical appearance? When your wash is complete, gently squeeze as much water out of your locs as possible. People often wring, or squeeze and twist, their locs to get all of the water out however that is very damaging to your locs. Over time, this will cause thinning and breakage. Remember to squeeze your locs without twisting to retain your hair's strength.

Once you finish gently squeezing out as much water as you can, then towel dry. I recommend you wrap your hair in a microfiber towel for up to 20-30 minutes. A microfiber towel will absorb water from your locs without transferring lint into your locs and without encouraging frizziness. If you can, allow your hair to air dry naturally. Artificial heat from blow dryers and overhead dryers can be very damaging over time. It may leave your hair brittle and more prone to breakage. If you want to begin minimizing your artificial heat usage, start by blow drying for a designated amount of time and air drying the rest until you feel comfortable eliminating artificial heat all together.

It's vital to make sure that your locs are able to dry completely or else your hair will become a breeding ground for mold and mildew. Make sure your hair has completely dried prior to covering your hair with hats and scarves to prevent mildew. If you've poorly dried your hair and are battling with mildew as a result, you may need to rewash your hair with a shampoo that has antibacterial components. Try adding tea tree oil to your shampoo. The sun kills mildew naturally so if you can, sit in the sun to dry your hair if you live in a warm climate or during warm weather months like May through September.

# ROOT MAINTENANCE

Most commonly, new growth and roots are maintained by twisting in a clockwise direction. This is typically done after each time locs are washed or after select washes, as desired. This is often referred to as grooming or retwisting. It is important to maintain the habit of twisting your roots in the same direction with each retwist. This will help bring uniformity to your loc's appearance. It will also help your hair lock as you are training it consistency. In the early stages of locking while your locs are still forming, it is very important to retwist after every single wash. This will help you train your locs to be one uniform shape without much inconsistencies.

Most people desire a very cylindrical shape in their locs, much like pencils or straws. Lack of regular retwisting may lead to lumpy locs or every flat locs. Of course, if you desire a more natural and organic loc appearance, consistent maintenance is not necessary.

While it is important for people with starter locs to retwist after each wash, it is also important for them to palm roll. Palm rolling is the act of rolling your locs in the palms of your hands. This will train your hair to loc in a cylindrical shape and reduce frizz which is often problematic during the early stages.

Many people choose to retwist their locs because of the sleek appearance after a fresh retwist and it provides a smooth and uniform appearance as the hair locs. A major con is the fact that contact with water or excess sweat will revert a fresh retwist back to its original loose natural state.

Retwisting isn't the only way you can maintain your roots. People often choose to interlock their roots. Interlocking is the act of using a tool to pull your locs through your roots to create knots to keep the hairs together. This method of grooming your roots will not come undone in the wash which makes it an attractive option. A con is that interlocking doesn't provide a sleek look, especially since interlocking can only be done once every couple of months since you need a significant amount of new growth to interlock without causing damage.

Choosing to interlock or retwist your roots is a matter of lifestyle and preference. No method is superior to the other. Regardless if you choose to retwist or to interlock, it is important to maintain your locs in the same direction. Lastly, of course your roots will lock on their own without the aid of retwisting or interlocking. Many people choose to freeform their locs as that is the most natural way to cultivate locs and it provides a thick and luscious appearance. A con is that society deems the freeform asthetic as "unkempt and unruly" however I recommend that you do what is right for you regardless of public opinion.

It is very common for hairs to accumulate in between locs. Sometimes those hairs marry each other, or lock together, causing multiple locs to attach at the root. This can be prevented and cured by regularly popping your locs. This is the act of snapping your locs apart so that you keep the integrity of your loc's parts and so your locs don't grow into one.

# MOISTURIZING

An extremely common issue with maintaining locs is moisture retention. People often complain about dry locs which is undesirable. Water is the number one source of moisture for hair so no matter how many products you apply to your hair; it will continue to have a dry feeling if you neglect to add water to your hair. Be sure to wash your hair regularly and mist your hair with a handy spray bottle as needed, avoiding your roots to not disrupt your retwist.

Rose water is a great source of moisture as well, especially considering the number of toxins that appears in our tap water. If you can, use a shower head and a faucet with a filter to get better water quality to wash and mist your hair. Many people have success with using water on their locs alone without using any products whatsoever. However, a lot of us cannot get our desired results with water alone, especially those of us who use heat to dry and set our hair or those of us who chemically treat our locs with bleach, permanent dyes and semi-permanent dyes. If water alone will suffice, that's awesome! If not, you may try different products to see which ones work well with your locs.

Avoid using heavy products on your locs and scalp. Greasy products tend to have petroleum as one of the primary ingredients. Petroleum is known to clog follicles and hinder hair growth. It is also very difficult to wash heavy products out of locs therefore causing product buildup. Many locticians will recommend not using products on your locs at all however many loc wearers prefer to do so anyway.

Should you decide to use products, I recommend using lightweight products with natural ingredients. Consider oils or water based pomades that penetrate the hair shaft as well as oils that coat the hair shaft to seal in moisture. Often a bit of experimentation with oils will help you determine which ones work best with your hair type.

# ITCHY SCALP

Regardless of what is our hairstyles of choice, we will experience an itchy scalp. Itchiness from time to time is normal but it becomes problematic when it persists and is constantly recurring. To cure an itchy scalp and to prevent an itchy scalp, it is important to understand the causes.

Dehydration can cause an itchy scalp. There are times when you may have neglected to drink the recommended amount of water. Remember that our skin, hair and nails are very often reflections of how we care for ourselves internally. So be sure to keep up your hydration so that you don't dry out your scalp.

Your scalp may be itchy because it may need to come into direct contact with water. You don't always have to wash it when it itches. Sometimes a light mist of water alone or mixed with oils, or rose water, can be a quick fix to an itchy scalp. After a light mist, a massage will feel amazing and may further aid in curing your itchy scalp.

Sometimes your scalp may itch because it is dirty. Often people think that to end the itchiness, you must apply some sort of anti-itch product to your scalp, like a carrier oil mixed with an essential oil. This can be a great solution but if done too often or too heavily, it can exacerbate the issue instead.

# HOT OIL TREATMENTS VS. CONDITIONERS

Both hot oil treatments and conditioners are used after washing as a way to help your hair retain moisture. Loc purists will steer clear of using conditioner on their locs as conditioner can potentially have dangerous ingredients, cause product build up as well as interrupt the locking process on immature locs due to its detangling nature. Some people are against hot oil treatments because of its likeness to frying due to heating up oil on your hair. However, the determining factor of whether or not you should use hot oil treatments or conditioner is up to your preference. I recommend the usage of both hot oil treatments and conditioners from time to time if you are fond of both moisture retention techniques.

For loc beginners, I must warn you that conditioners can very well reverse the process, especially if your locs haven't begun to bud. Just as I recommended earlier, if you decide to condition your starter locs, try using a stocking cap to keep your locs intact. The stocking cap may cause more difficulty washing out the conditioner fully in comparison to washing out the shampoo so I advise that you have someone look through your hair to help point out spots that you missed and then wash those individual locs in the sink outside of the stocking cap with low water pressure. Should you decide to do a hot oil treatment, you may have better results at this stage in your loc journey. An easy way to hot oil treat your locs is by misting your locs, oiling them and putting them inside a plastic shower cap. Getting into the shower will steam your hair, providing a simple and easy alternative to heating up oil or heating up a moist towel for a traditional hot oil treatment.

# BEDTIME MAINTENANCE

The way that you sleep with your locs at night will play a major role in how your locs look during the daytime. There are many ways that you can cover your hair and/or edges for bed to maintain a neat appearance. Every single method includes silk or satin material. Satin is most common as it is most inexpensive so I'll keep referencing satin in this chapter. Satin is an ideal material for bedtime maintenance because it keeps the moisture in your hair while materials like cotton suck the moisture out of your hair, leaving it dry and brittle come morning. It also helps hair stay soft and smooth as well as keep your retwist intact.

A couple of classic ways people go to sleep are in satin scarves and bonnets. If you have long hair, you may want to put your locs in a bun or ponytail, fold the square satin scarf into a large triangle and then tie your hair completely inside of the scarf. To alleviate some of the tension on your scalp, you may opt to leave your hair down and simply tie the scarf around your edges. In this case, your locs are exposed but your edges will be smooth and intact. Bonnets are great options for securing your locs and protecting them from exposure but they aren't as effective at smoothening your edges. However, you can absolutely use a bonnet in conjunction with a scarf to completely cover your hair and smooth your edges.

Many people are prone to getting headaches due to wearing tight scarves while others can't seem to keep their satin scarves on their heads throughout the night at all. If either applies to you, you may want to consider sleeping on satin sheets and satin pillowcases. This way, your hair won't come into significant contact with cotton all night long and it will retain its moisture.

# TOP 3 LOC ENEMIES: PRODUCT BUILD-UP, LINT & FRIZZ

## PRODUCT BUILD-UP

If you ask people with locs what their biggest struggles are with their loc maintenance, the answers will be close to unanimous. Product build-up is a major headache for loc wearers. What is product build-up? Product build up is left over product that remains in your locs after washing as it isn't easily washed out of your hair during your regular wash routine. This happens when you use the wrong products that are too heavy for your hair. It also happens when you don't wash your locs as often as you need to considering the amount of products you put in your locs, or if you use the wrong shampoo or conditioner and/or don't wash it out fully.

Often when you use too much of a product, it attracts dust and dirt to your hair and if you're not careful, it can get cemented into your hair over time. Product build-up can weigh your hair down, making it feel heavier. It can also give your hair a grey and dusty appearance, especially under flash photography. Product build up is gross.

To prevent product build up, make sure you wet your hair thoroughly before applying shampoo or conditioner to allow the product to be evenly distributed throughout your locs and not get stuck at one section. I recommend that you use lightweight shampoo and conditioner or dilute the product to a thinner consistency so that it is easily washed out and not left behind. When rinsing the shampoo and conditioner out of your locs, be sure to massage your locs and scalp thoroughly to make sure there is no product left behind. Pay special attention to the part of your locs where your loose new growth meet your locked hair as that is a spot where shampoo and/or conditioner is commonly left behind. When you feel as though you have washed your hair out thoroughly enough, rinse it again. And then rinse it again.

Whether you choose to use all natural products or not, be sure to not use too much product to avoid product build up. Although you may love the smell, the feelings, the ingredients and their uses, it may not be necessary at all to use more than recommended on the label. Often less is more. This applies to shampoo, conditioner, gel, oils, creams, lotions, serums, mists, hair deodorizers, etc. Products that are water and oil based will wash out a lot easier than products that are based in petroleum. Pay close attention to the first three ingredients on the ingredients list as those are most abundant in the product. Greases and butters are difficult to fully wash out. I do not recommend the usage of greases at all but everyone has their preferences. Butters, such as shea butter, are great for natural hair however it can be too heavy for locs if used too often. Limit your usage of greases and butters if you choose to use them at all; make sure to use them in moderation.

Perhaps you made a few mistakes and now you have product build up. Getting rid of product build up is not nearly as easy as it is to cause the build-up in the first place. But have no fear, dirty locs are not a death sentence. You can fully clean your locs over a period of time using the right methods. One method is the ever popular Apple Cider Vinegar (ACV) rinse. There are many ways to do this rinse but I'll discuss one simple way.

Fill up a tub, basin or a stopped sink with warm water. Add about 1 cup of apple cider vinegar into the water and mix well. You can soak your locs in this solution alone or you can add in a few table spoons of baking soda, sea salt and/or lemon juice. Soak your locs in the mixture and massage gently yet thoroughly. You can also massage your problem areas while soaking to ensure that the build-up is loosened so that it can be rinsed out. After several minutes, you'll notice the water turning to a murky color. This is a good sign because you can see the dirt and build up is being removed. Make sure you rinse out your locs after the soak until the water runs clear. Be mindful that if you choose to use this method while your hair is dyed with a semi-permanent hair color, you may notice that your color will be rinsed out significantly. This method of deep cleaning locs should only be used once every few months as it can be very drying.

As a heads up, many people have had negative results with ACV rinses. This is typically because the rinse brought the product build up to the surface and not all the way out of the locs, leaving the locs with a dirtier appearance than originally. In this case, I would recommend the usage of anti-residue and anti-build up shampoos as I have reviewed on my YouTube channel. These types of shampoos can be very drying if used too frequently so I recommend that you use them once every few washes or use them consistently only in the event of obvious product build up.

# LINT

Lint is a nuisance that can be overwhelming to deal with. Unlike with product build-up, it cannot be washed out with multiple deep cleanses. Prevention is far better than cure regarding lint and locs for sure. This nemesis must be handled strategically and not with haste or impulse.

Loc wearers tend to accumulate lint in their locs from their hair brushing up against their shirts and sweaters, resting on old linty bedding and pillow cases, sweeping and dusting lint particles into the air and into their locs while cleaning up around the house, etc.

Our best bet in avoiding lint from ever getting into contact with our locs is by covering our hair while going to sleep, while cleaning and by avoiding old wooly and linty clothing. Implementing some of the suggestions in the bedtime chapter will help you keep locs free of lint for sure. Maybe you don't want to get rid of your favorite ugly Christmas sweater, that's perfectly fine, but perhaps you can wear your hair up in a bun so that your locs aren't brushing against the sweater that day.

One of the ways that lint gets imbedded into your locs is by washing your locs. Remember, water helps your hair lock and it also helps lint to lock into your hair. Before washing your locs, simply give your locs a nice thorough shake to rid of any lint that may be on the very surface of your locs. You can also use a soft bristle brush and brush your locs prior to washing. This will remove any lint that is on the surface and any lint that is beginning to lock into your hair. Since loc brushing can interrupt the locking process for immature locs, brushing should only be done on locs that are at least 2 years mature. I would suggest that you brush your locs no closer than 3 or 4 inches to the scalp. Keep in mind that no matter if you've been locking your hair for 10 years, the hair closer to your scalp is still immature. Brushing immature locs can lead to unraveling and excess frizz.

Lint also gets imbedded into locs through the process of drying them. Using old linty towels to dry your locs can easily transfer tons of lint into your locs. Avoiding the usage of light colored towels and old towels to dry your hair will significantly limit the amount of lint you experience in your locs. Microfiber towels are also recommended as they don't build up lint the way towels with your average fibers do so there really isn't any lint on the towel to transfer into your locs this way.

Once lint has been imbedded fully into your loc, one of the worst things you can do is begin to pick at it with your finger nails. I've noticed this practice causes breakage and thinning at the spot where the lint now lives. This is because our fingers are too big and nails are too sharp to effectively pull out stubborn lint. We'll get a better grip at the lint by using a pair of tweezers although this must be done with great precision and care because this method can still cause damage if done incorrectly.

Sometimes our prevention techniques are inadequate and we have an unlucky encounter. In this case, we may need to resort to dying our locs to minimize or eliminate the appearance of lint. If you dye your hair regularly this may not be an issue but if your hair is your natural color, you may want to consider dying your hair all over for a change or getting the perfect shade of dye to match your natural hair color and dying the problem areas alone. The choice is yours.

# FRIZZ

No matter where you are in your loc journey, you will battle with frizz. Whether it is an issue is up to one's preference but in general, even those individuals who like their frizziness still want to be able to limit the frizz for special occasions sometimes. Here are some useful ways on how to prevent, cure and tame frizzy locs:

1) Wash Locs with Cool Water
   - Avoid washing your hair with water that is really high in temperature. This may sound daunting for some of you who wash their hair in the shower. It isn't absolutely necessary to use cold water during the wash however it is recommended to use cool water for your final rinse. Hot water encourages frizz while cool water helps to settle it.

2) Dry Your Locs with Microfiber Towels or Cotton T-Shirts
   - Towels with regular fibers encourage frizz while using a microfiber towel or a cotton t-shirt are great at smoothening frizz. Microfiber towels and cotton t-shirts may not be as

effective at absorbing water as regular towels but keeping a couple of towels or cotton tees is recommended to absorb all of the water you can.

3) Palm Rolling
    - Regular palm rolling after you wash your locs will help the frizz settle down into the loc and reduce frizz. Even if you don't retwist your roots during regular maintenance, you can still place your loc(s) in the palm of your hand and rub your hands together in short quick strokes, back and forth to settle the frizz. This should be done after every wash for the best results. Refrain from palm rolling dry hair which can cause breakage.

4) Gel
    - Using a bit of gel or another pomade will help to reduce frizz. While hair is damp, apply a little gel to your loc prior to palm rolling. This will be a more effective method than palm rolling alone. Using gel will provide a firmer hold which will last longer and provide a more manicured appearance.

5) Bedtime Maintenance
    - Wrapping up your hair in satin and silk scarves to go to bed will greatly reduce frizz. Frizz is often caused by dryness and these materials help your hair retain moisture. You can also use satin or silk pillowcases and/or sheets to keep the moisture in your hair and prevent frizz.

6) Avoid Cotton Hair Ties/Accessories
    - Cotton is a very absorbent material. It is good at drawing moisture out of hair which is good for drying your hair after washing but it is problematic to wear on dry hair. Cotton scarves, laying on cotton pillow cases and using cotton hair accessories will all draw out some natural and added moisture from your locs resulting in frizz. Steer clear of using cotton around your edges as these hairs tend to be the easiest to break off from dryness.

7) Protective Styling
    - Protective styles such as buns, braids and twists keep your hair secure and compact. These styles are best for

keeping your locs tucked away so that you can leave them alone for extended periods of time. With them being secured, they don't require much manipulation or contact with anything that will encourage frizz. Constant hair touching alone can create frizzy locs. Also, compact styles pack down the frizz, especially when the style has been in for an extended amount of time. Frizz can develop on the surface of your updo if you do not follow through with appropriate maintenance. I suggest you remember to wrap your hair in a satin scarf to keep your protective style fresh and keep the frizz matted down.

8) Regular Maintenance
    - Developing a routine that you stick to will help you learn your hair. You'll be able to learn what your hair likes, what it hates and what it requires for your hair to have your desired look and feel. It is wise to keep track of your frizziest times, like when you forget to use a shower cap in the bath. Knowing ahead of time when your hair needs to be maintained is especially crucial if you

have an event to go to and you need impeccable frizz free hair. With the advanced knowledge of when your hair tends to get the frizziest, which is typically soon before you are due for a washing and grooming or when you are dealing with shifts in the weather, you can plan accordingly.

9) Limit Usage of Artificial Heat
- Often times, frizz is the result of heat damage caused by over usage or improper usage of artificial heat from blow dryers and over the head dryers. Such heat will permanently straighten naturally curly hair causing some hairs to stick out of your locs. To prevent this type of frizz, air dry your locs as often as you can. Go for a walk or sit in the sun if the weather permits. During the moments when time is of the essence, use low heat and hold the heat 6-12 inches away from your hair.

10) Avoid or Limit Hair Dyes
- Similarly, to artificial heat, hair dyes can cause damage which can permanently alter the texture of one's hair resulting in hairs sticking out of one's locs. Limit the amount of times

you dye your locs to prevent this occurrence. Try to only dye your new growth instead of re-dying previously colored locs. If you feel the need to refresh your hair color all over, try to use semi-permanent dyes instead as they are gentler on hair. Avoid dying your locs before they are fully locked. Immature locs are already frizzy in nature so adding on more frizz as a result of dye damage is highly undesirable.

11) Bonus: Patience
- Remember that frizz is an inevitable part of your loc journey. When your locs are beginning to lock, this may be your frizziest time. This is completely normal and should be expected. Continue doing regular maintenance but refrain from over-manipulating your locs at this stage to ensure proper and healthy locking. With patience, your locs will prosper.

# LUMPS

Lumps are a natural feature of a loc journey. I want to say lumps are inevitable but there are some people whose locs are completely smooth, uniformed and manicured. That does not represent the vast majority of us though. Most of us will encounter a lump in the road or many lumps for that matter. Lumps typically don't indicate any issues with your locs. They are very common during the immature stages of the locking process as locs do not form all at once.

Your locs may appear and feel lumpy because of budding and because your hair is locking more at different parts of your locs. Mature locs may also experience lumps, especially in more organic locs formed with less frequent manipulation. These lumps however, can be smoothed out over time with regular palm rolling on the lump. It is a common practice to simply use your thumb and index finger to imitate palm rolling concentrated on the lump. This activity over time will encourage loc lumps to subside.

If your lump is caused by hair breakage where broken hair has gathered together in a knot, that can be a sign of excess stress at the thin spot. This is often a result of breakage at the root. If this is the case, it is important to assess why breakage is occurring at your root. It may be due to health problems so it is important to have regular physical examinations and maintain your health and wellness daily. Lumps due to breakage can also happen throughout the length of the loc if it experiences constant and excess stress at the same spot. Give your hair regular breaks from tension causing styles so that your styles don't cause irreversible damage to your locs.

# THINNING, BREAKAGE & BALD SPOTS

One of the scariest things to deal with is thinning locs which lead to breakage. Breakage can occur at the most inconvenient of times so it is important to be aware of thinning locs before they break so that you can treat it accordingly. Thinning occurs as a result of over manipulation such as retwisting and styling too often, too tightly and/or while dry. Retwisting no more frequently than once every 2 weeks is a general rule that many loc'd wearers go by. However upon learning your hair, you may find that your hair can tolerate being twisted slightly more often or you may discover that once every 2 weeks is too frequent for you.

Upon learning your hair, you will find a frequency that works best for you. You will discover how often your hair and scalp can tolerate styling as well upon learning your hair. While improper retwisting may result in thinning at the root, over styling can result in thinning anywhere in the length of the loc. Going back and forth from proper retwisting to improper retwisting can result in thinning throughout the length of the loc as the hair grows out.

It is safe to say that the overwhelming majority of loc wearers will agree that one should never retwist their hair while dry. Firstly, your retwist will not be very effective whatsoever if it's been twisted without moisture. Secondly, dry retwisting is a surefire way to cause breakage at the root. People with hand-in-hair syndrome may experience breakage due to dryness as well. I recommend that when you play in your hair, or even when you are simply taking down a set of braids or twists, you should moisturize your fingers first with oil and/or water. The consistent friction of your dry fingertips and even your nails can cause unwanted breakage. I also recommend that if you are styling your locs, mist your hair with some water first so that your hair is more malleable and the friction is reduced.

Repairing thinning is a lot harder than preventing it so do the best you can to keep your hair healthy. One method of repairing thin spots is by placing a series of knots on the affected area to reinforce it. You may end up losing about an inch of length on that particular loc but you will regain your locs strength and uniformity, at least temporarily. Some people choose to reinforce thin spots by adding fake hair to the affected area, with synthetic or human hair. Adding thread will strengthen the thin section as well and lastly and most simply, trimming the loc below the thin spot will prevent it from breaking off on its own and creating an embarrassing moment.

Balding may occur for different reasons so it is vital to discover what is causing the balding in the first place. A visit to the dermatologist may be in order as it could potentially be a health concern. It is very common for the root cause (pun intended) of the baldness to be due to traction alopecia which is hair loss due to over manipulation and improper styling as mentioned above. This can be permanent hair loss but is often reversible. Oils that are often used to help thicken hair include the carrier oil, castor oil and the essential oil, clove oil.

While re-growing bald spots may take a significant amount of time, you can achieve the look of a filled bald spot by applying hair-like fibers to it for a realistic look or you can easily apply eyeliner or eyeshadow to the bald spot for a temporary fill while you are still regularly using your oils for regrowth.

# HAIRLINE AND EDGES CARE

One common insecurity regarding black hair is the state of your hairline and your edges. Many people struggle with receding hairlines, thinning, frizzy and dry edges. Apart from extreme circumstances, these issues can be resolved and prevented with care and effort. Alopecia is a condition that may require medical attention so if you believe you may be experiencing permanent hair loss, a trip to a dermatologist may be necessary.

Receding hairlines are often the result of over retwisting and over interlocking. Retwists generally should not be done more frequently than once every two weeks and interlocking should only be done once every few months. Manipulating the hair on your hairline while dry can also cause breakage and result in a receding hairline. If you are not maintaining damp hair that has been freshly washed, keep a spray bottle handy so that you can dampen the hair prior to twisting and tight styling so that there is not a lot of pressure on the root and scalp. Jamaican Black Castor Oil is widely used for encouraging the regrowth and strengthening of edges. Do not pull your hair back in a tight bun or ponytail very often to protect your hairline.

Sometimes our hairline needs a break. From time to time, refrain from grooming your hairline to give it a chance to grow back and fill in. Simply wear a satin scarf around your edges so that you are able to retain moisture during sleep, as the lack of moisture can cause breakage and damage your hairline. Be cautious when taking your breaks from retwisting because that can often result in the flattening of your locs. If flattening occurs, keep up with your regular palm rolling to keep your cylindrical shape.

# EXERCISE

For those of us who like to exercise regularly, exercising can be a major concern for loc wearers due to the amount of sweat one's scalp may excrete. Excess sweat may cause retwisted roots to unravel. It may also call for washing far more often than normal. If you fall into any of these categories, you will benefit greatly from interlocking your hair rather than retwisting. Interlocked hair will not unravel due to sweat or frequent washes because the technique crotchets the hair together. The downside of this method is that interlocking should only be done once every several months so your roots will have a chance to grow out.

If you choose not to interlock your hair, you can maintain a fresh retwist by keeping your hair wrapped tightly in a satin scarf during your workout. Keep the scarf on after your workout until your sweat dries on its own. The downside to this technique is that you are avoiding washing your locs when you may need to.

Whether you choose to interlock or tie up your hair, protective styles will be very helpful when it comes to maintaining locs as an individual who exercises a lot. Styles like braids and twists can be worn during exercise and even rinsed afterwards with the styles intact. This is also a great way to maintain your locs in the summertime, as a swimmer and as a life guard.

# HAIR COLOR

Please be advised that no matter if you go to a professional for your dye job or if you dye your hair yourself using a box dye, there is no guarantee that you will get your desired results. Also, please keep in mind that when dying your locs, you are working with harmful chemicals that damage your hair, so prepare for potential irreversible damage that may come from improper usage, over usage and poor aftercare.

Being that the roots of your hair are virgin hair, your roots will take to color quickest and may produce the most vibrant results. Therefore, it is often best to color your hair from ends to roots. I recommend heavily coating your locs with the dye so that you get a very consistent color though out your hair. I do not recommend squeezing the dye into the locs because it is unnecessary for the dye to reach the core of the loc as only the surface hairs are visible. Plus, it gets very difficult to wash out dye, or any product, once it's deep in your locs.

I advise that you thoroughly wash the dye out of your hair. Dye, as well as bleach, that is deep into your loc and not washed out, may eat away at your loc over time and cause thinning and breakage. When washing color out of your locs, keep rinsing until the water runs clear. This will help reduce bleeding on clothing, sheets and other fabrics.

To maintain vibrant colored hair, wash your hair with cool temperature water. Hot water will cause more bleeding thus more fading. You can also use shampoo for color treated hair or for your specific dyed color.

Lastly, when chemically treating your hair, it is important to maintain its moisture. Hot oil treatments and/or deep conditions are great ways to combat dryness which commonly affects people with locs.

# 10 TIPS FOR HAIR GROWTH

### 1) Eat Well and Drink Water

This is perhaps the most obvious tip for growing long healthy hair. The things you put inside your body are reflected in your appearance, especially your skin, nails and of course your hair.

### 2) Supplements

For those of us who do not eat as well as we should, supplements are a great addition to our daily routine. There are specific supplements in the market that you can take that encourage long and healthy hair growth.

### 3) Exfoliating Your Scalp

Due to the products that we apply to our scalps and the flakes that accumulate, exfoliating your scalp is highly recommended to encourage hair growth. Products and flakes can be barriers that hinder hair growth.

### 4) Avoid Scratching Scalp

Scratching your scalp excessively can damage your hair follicles and hinder hair growth. Rather than using your nails to scratch your scalp, use your fingertips to rub the itch away.

### 5) Avoid Petroleum

This heavy grease coats the scalp and prevents it from breathing. It creates product buildup that discourage healthy hair growth.

### 6) Carrier Oils and Essential Oils

Oils are lighter than petroleum and hair responds to oils very well. Try using your favorite carrier oil with a few drops of your favorite essential oil that stimulate blood circulation to encourage healthy hair growth.

### 7) Scalp Massages

Massages, especially when paired with a nice mix of oils, do very well at stimulating hair growth. You can even stand up and bend over to boost blood flow to your scalp while massaging.

### 8) Don't Over Wash Your Hair

Washing your hair too frequently dries out your scalp and hair. The sebum that our scalps produce encourage healthy growth so it is necessary to find out how often is appropriate to wash your own hair.

### 9) Protective Styles

Protective styles allow your scalp and roots to rest, thus reducing the breakage that may occur from frequent manipulation.

### 10) Reduce Artificial Heat

Artificial heat may cause breakage in excess. Breakage will hinder length retention so using a cooler setting on your blow dryer will be beneficial.

# LOC REMOVAL

May you all have blessed loc journeys. I hope that you are able to learn all that you needed to learn about your hair and your selves. Should you decide to end your journey, there are a few ways you can go about doing so.

The most obvious solution to ending a loc journey is cutting off your locs. Many people come to regret cutting their locs off sooner or later afterwards. For this reason, I highly recommend saving your locs in case you decide to have them reattached. Many locticians offer great reattachment services.

Faux locs and loc extensions are very popular nowadays. You can potentially donate or sell your locs to be used as extensions if you cut your locs off and save them.

Many people choose to comb their locs out. The longer and more mature your locs are, the more difficult it would be to comb them out. Combing out locs is also very hard on a comb so I recommend trying to use a metal fork if you end up dealing with breaking combs. Keep in mind that combing out long locs will be very time consuming.

Since the ends of the locs are the oldest and most locked, I recommend cutting the locs halfway prior to combing them out. This way the locs will be more easily combed out and the loose natural hair you are left with will be stronger and healthier.

# GLOSSARY

Here are some of the terms I may have used throughout this book, defined by myself or an official dictionary, for your better understanding.

1) **Alopecia**- the partial or complete absence of hair from areas of the body where it normally grows (Oxford Dictionaries)
2) **Backcombing**- the act of combing a section of hair up towards the roots to instantly mat the hair to form locs. Very often the method of starting locs for people with straighter hair textures.
3) **Braidlocs**- formed from braids matting together into locs.
4) **Carrier oils**- these oils are vegetable based and are often used to dilute concentrated essential oils
5) **Comb coils**- spring-like coils formed with a fine-toothed comb, very often the starter style of loc formation for kinky textures.
6) **Essential oils**- highly concentrated oils extracted from plants for medicinal uses, auromatherapy and for fragrance. To be mixed with carrier oils for topical use.
7) **Faux locs** (pronounced 'foh'-locs)- hair extensions that give the illusion of natural locs for a temporary protective style.

8) **Freeforming-** the method of forming locs without manipulation such as parting and twisting. The most organic method of cultivating locs.
9) **Interlocking-** to crotchet hair to form locs or groom new growth.
10) **Instant locs-** locs that are partially formed upon installation with a crotchet needle or another like tool.
11) A. **Locs**(noun)- a narrow ropelike strand of hair formed by matting or braiding. (Merriam-Webster dictionary)
    B. **Loc**(verb)- the act of a loc(noun) forming. Also spelled "lock" (past participle: loc'd)
12) **Loctician-** a hairstylist that specializes in maintaining and styling locs.
13) **Loc journey-** Often recognized to be the time from starting one's locs to the time when they are fully locked. It is also often recognized as the time from when one begins the locking process to the time one cuts their locs off or combs them out. This period represents growth in the literal sense regarding hair, and growth in the figurative sense regarding the individual in a personal or spiritual level.
14) **Loc popping-** the separation of the locs that begin to tangle at the root so that they do not marry. Pulling the locs apart creates the popping sound.

15) **Loose natural**- afro hair that is not locked or an individual with afro hair that is not locked.
16) **Marrying locs**- the act of two or more locs, either on their own or by force, combining to form a thicker loc.
17) **Naturalista**- A beautiful woman who embraces and flaunts her natural curls through trendy and classy styles.
18) **Palmroll**- the act of rolling locs in one's palm to settle frizz and give locs a uniform cylindrical shape.
19) **Product build-up**- the accumulation of product residue in one's hair.
20) **Pruning**- cutting stubborn hairs sticking out of the loc to give a neater, more maintained appearance.
21) **Retwist**- loc maintenance involving the twisting of new growth. The most common method of grooming locs.
22) **Semipermanent dye**- dye that chemically alters the color of hair for a set amount of washes. After a certain amount of washes, the color fades away.
23) **Shrinkage**- the recoil of curly hair.
24) **Sebum**- the natural oil that skin produces.
25) **Traction alopecia**- alopecia caused from too much tight manipulation from styles such as braids, twists, etc.
26) **Virgin hair**- natural hair that has not been dyed or chemically processed.

# ABOUT THE AUTHOR

Peace! I am Keisha Charmaine, best known for being a loc enthusiast. I create tutorials available for free on my YouTube channel and I post inspirational hair photos on my Instagram profile. I love encouraging those struggling with accepting their natural locked hair as beautiful. I began my YouTube channel to document my loc journey and soon enough it evolved into a channel where I help locked naturals maintain their hair throughout troubling stages and situations throughout their loc journeys.

Oh? Did you want to learn about me as a person? Well, I'm a Pisces, born March 6th and my life path number is master number 11. I am a deep thinker, very spiritual and intuitive. I greatly value my alone time but am very friendly and easy to get along with. I call myself a social loner. I am a sweetheart, very loving and giving but I am very assertive and sassy. I am a creative; I love to write, draw, dance and sing (although I don't sing very well.) I love to laugh and smile and be goofy. I am the type to listen to music while riding the train, mouthing the words, nodding my head, tapping my feet and dancing in my seat, without a care of who's watching, and trust me, they're watching. When I have, I give, because I know **I am blessed** and more will always be replenished.

# THANK YOU

I would like to give a special thanks to all the amazing women who contributed quotes which are featured throughout Part 1. Thank you, friends, family, peers and fellow loc influencers. Your contributions are a meaningful addition for which I am ever-so grateful.

Jenelle Nurse, Jasmine Andrews, Tai McLeod, Destinee Lloyd, Brittany Lingard, Gina Riggins, Elizabeth Paul, Dominique Harrison, Ruqayyah Batts, Renee Edwards, Monique Collins, Monet Collins, Tyree V., Kimberley Smith, Julia Satin, Rukayatu Tijani, sapoDILLA, Ieasha Tiffany, Liz R., Danielle Loxs, Rii Fitzgerald-Fields, Nardia Brown, Sawdayah Brownlee, Shana Boatswain, Mandy Mc., Denequa Williams & Nay Marie.

Thank you, mommy for your patience in editing and thank you, Dr. Chirwa for reviewing my work. Thank you Chioma for taking my photos last summer and fall. Thank you, Curtis for your graphic artwork.

Thank you, God for never giving up on me!

CPSIA information can be obtained
at www.ICGtesting.com
Printed in the USA
FFOW03n0655040817
38498FF